WALKS IN THE
DORDOGNE

Titles in the Footpaths of Europe Series

Normandy and the Seine
Walking through Brittany
Walks in Provence
Coastal Walks: Normandy and Brittany
Walking the Pyrenees
Walks in the Auvergne
Walks in the Dordogne
Walks in the Loire Valley
Walking the GR5: Modane to Larche
Walking the GR5: Lake Geneva to Mont-Blanc
Paris to Boulogne
Walks in Corsica

The publishers thank the following people for permission to use their photographs in this book: J. Cantaloube, H. Viaux, J. M. Humeau, D. Fortunato.

WALKS IN THE DORDOGNE

Translated by Charles Polley
in association with First Edition

Robertson McCarta

The publishers thank the following people for their help with this book: Isabelle
Daguin, Philippe Lambert, Serge Sineux, Daphne Terry

First published in 1990 by

Robertson McCarta Limited
122 King's Cross Road,
London WC1X 9DS

in association with

Fédération Française de Randonnée Pédestre
8 Avenue Marceau
75008 Paris

© Robertson McCarta Limited
© Fédération Française de Randonnée Pédestre
© Maps, Institut Geographique National (French Official Survey)
   and Robertson McCarta Limited.

Managing Editor Folly Marland
Series designed by Prue Bucknall
Production by Grahame Griffiths
Typeset by Columns Limited, Reading
Planning Map by Rodney Paull

Printed and bound in Spain by Graficas Estella S.A.

British Library Cataloguing in Publication Data

Walks in the Dordogne — (Footpaths of Europe)
   1. France. Dordogne. Visitors' guides
   I. Series
   914.4'7204838

   ISBN 1–85365–104–4

Every care has been taken to ensure that all the information in this
book is accurate. The publishers cannot accept any responsibility
for any errors that may appear or their consequences.

CONTENTS

IGN map legend   6
From the publisher   7
Key   8
The footpaths of France, introduction by Robin Neillands   9
The Dordogne, introduction   15

The walks and maps

Walk 1   25

GR36 Angouleme ▶ Les Eyzies-de-Tayac
GR436 Detour ▶ La Mazaurie
GR461 Detour ▶ Terrasson-la-Villedieu

Walk 2   75

GR6 Les Eyzies-de-Tayac ▶ Monbazillac
GR36 Monbazillac ▶ Cahors

Walk 3   107

GR36, GR46 Cahors and the Tour des Gorges de l'Aveyron

Walk 4   169

GR65, GR651 Cahors ▶ Figeac
GR6 Figeac ▶ Les Eyzies-de-Tayac

Accommodation guide   210
Index   215

Key to IGN Maps

Motorway, dual carriageway

Major road, four lanes or more

Main road, two-lane or three-lane, wide

Main road, two-lane, narrow

Narrow road, regularly surfaced

Principal — Secondary

Other narrow road: regularly surfaced: irregularly surfaced

Possibly private or controlled access

Field track, forest track, felling track, footpath

Track of disused road. Road under construction

Road through embankment, cutting. Tree-lined road or track

Bank. Hedge, line of trees

Railway: double track, single track. Electrified line. Station, waiting line. Halt, stop

Sidings or access lines. Narrow gauge line. Rack railway

Electricity transmission line. Cable railway. Ski lift

National boundary with markers

Boundary and administrative centre of department, district — PF — SP

Boundary and administrative centre of canton, commune — CT — C

For shooting times, go to town hall or gendarmerie

Boundary of military camp, firing range — x — x — x x — x

Boundary of State forest, National Park, outer zone of National Park

Triangulation points

Church, chapel, shrine. Cross, tomb, religious statue. Cemetery

Watch tower, fortress. Windmill, wind-pump. Chimney — Tr — Chem.

Storage tank: oil, gas. Blast furnace. Pylon. Quarry

Cave. Monument, pillar. Castle. Ruins — Mon. — P.V.

Megalithic monument, dolmen, menhir. Viewpoint. Campsite

Market-hall, shed, glasshouse, casemate

Access to underground workings. Refuge. Ski-jump — Mine — Cave

Population/thousands — 183,2 — 0,4 — 0,15 — 0,06

Bridge. Footbridge. Ford. Ferry

Lake, pool. Area liable to flooding. Marsh

Source, spring. Well, water-tank. Water-tower, reservoir — Ch$^{\underline{au}}$ d'Eau

Watercourse lined with trees. Waterfall. Dam. Dyke

Navigable canal, feeder or irrigator. Lock, machine-operated. Underground channel

Contour lines, 10 m. interval. Hollow. Small basin. Scree

Woodland   Scrub   Orchard, plantation   Vines   Ricefield

A note from the publisher

The books in this French Walking Guide series are published in association and with the help of the Fédération Française de la Randonnée Pédestre (French ramblers' association) — generally known as the FFRP.

The FFRP is a federal organisation and is made up of regional, local and many other associations and bodies that form its constituent parts. Individual membership is through these various local organisations. The FFRP therefore acts as an umbrella organisation overseeing the waymarking of footpaths, training and the publishing of the Topoguides, detailed guides to the Grande Randonnée footpaths.

There are at present about 170 Topoguides in print, compiled and written by local members of the FFRP, who are responsible for waymarking the walks — so they are well researched and accurate.

We have translated the main itinerary descriptions, amalgamating and adapting several Topoguides to create new regional guides. We have retained the basic Topoguide structure, indicating length and times of walks, and the Institut Géographique National (official French survey) maps overlaid with the routes.

The information contained in this guide is the latest available at the time of going to print. However, as publishers we are aware that this kind of information is continually changing and we are anxious to enhance and improve the guides as much as possible. We encourage you to send us suggestions, criticisms and those little bits of information you may wish to share with your fellow walkers. Our address is: Robertson-McCarta, 122 King's Cross Road, London WC1X 9DS.

We shall be happy to offer a free copy of any one of these books to any reader whose suggestions are subsequently incorporated into a new edition.

It is possible to create a variety of routes by referring to the walks in the Contents page and to the planning map (inside the front cover). Transport is listed in the alphabetical index at the back of the book and there is an accommodation guide.

KEY

Gournay

This example shows that it is 7km from Gournay to Arbois, and that you can expect it to take 2 hours, 10 minutes.

7Km
2:10

ARBOIS
⌂ ▲ ✕ ⚒ ▬
14th century church

Arbois has a variety of facilities, including hotels and buses. Hotel addresses and bus/train connections may be listed in the index at the back of the book.

a grey arrow indicates an alternative route that leaves and returns to the main route.

Detour

indicates a short detour off the route to a town with facilities or to an interesting sight.

Symbols:

⌂ hotel;
⌂ youth hostel, hut or refuge;
▲ camping;
✕ restaurant;
♈ cafe;

⚒ shops;
▬ railway station;
▬ buses;
▲ ferry;
i tourist information.

8

THE FOOTPATHS OF FRANCE

by Robin Neillands

Why should you go walking in France? Well, walking is fun and as for France, Danton summed up the attractions of that country with one telling phrase: 'Every man has two countries,' he said, 'his own . . . and France.' That is certainly true in my case and I therefore consider it both a pleasure and an honour to write this general introduction to these footpath guides to France. A pleasure because walking in or through France is my favourite pastime, an honour because these excellent English language guides follow in the course set by those Topo-guides published in French by the Fédération Française pour la Randonnée Pédestre, which set a benchmark for quality that all footpath guides might follow. Besides, I believe that good things should be shared and walking in France is one of the most pleasant activities I know.

I have been walking in France for over thirty years. I began by rambling — or rather ambling — through the foothills of the Pyrenees, crossing over into Spain past the old Hospice de France, coming back over the Somport Pass in a howling blizzard, which may account for the fact that I totally missed two sets of frontier guards on both occasions. Since then I have walked in many parts of France and even from one end of it to the other, from the Channel to the Camargue, and I hope to go on walking there for many years to come.

The attractions of France are legion, but there is no finer way to see and enjoy them than on foot. France has two coasts, at least three mountain ranges — the Alps, Pyrenees and the Massif Central — an agreeable climate, a great sense of space, good food, fine wines and, believe it or not, a friendly and hospitable people. If you don't believe me, go there on foot and see for yourself. Walking in France will appeal to every kind of walker, from the day rambler to the backpacker, because above all, and in the nicest possible way, the walking in France is well organised, but those Francophiles who already know France well, will find it even more pleasureable if they explore their favourite country on foot.

The GR system

The Grande Randonnée (GR) footpath network now consists of more than 40,000 kilometres (25,000 miles) of long-distance footpath, stretching into every part of France, forming a great sweep around Paris, probing deeply into the Alps, the Pyrenees, and the volcanic cones of the Massif Central. This network, the finest system of footpaths in Europe, is the creation of that marvellously named organisation, *la Fédération Française de Randonnée Pédestre, Comité National des Sentiers de Grande Randonnée*, which I shall abbreviate to FFRP-CNSGR. Founded in 1948, and declaring that, *'un jour de marche, huit jours de santé,'* the FFRP-CNSGR has flourished for four decades and put up the now familiar red-and-white waymarks in every corner of the country. Some of these footpaths are classic walks, like the famous GR65, *Le Chemin de St Jacques*, the ancient Pilgrim Road to Compostela, the TMB, the *Tour du Mont Blanc*, which circles the mountain through France, Switzerland and Italy, or the 600-mile long GR3, the *Sentier de la Loire*, which runs from the Ardèche to the Atlantic, to give three examples from the hundred or so GR trails available. In addition there is an abundance of GR du Pays or regional footpaths, like the *Sentier de la Haute Auvergne*, and the *Sentier Tour des Monts d'Aubrac*. A 'Tour' incidentally, is usually a circular walk. Many of these regional or provincial GR trails are charted and waymarked in red-and-yellow by local outdoor organisations such as ABRI (Association Bretonne des Relais et Itineraires) for Brittany, or CHAMINA for the Massif Central. The walker in France will soon become familiar with all these footpath networks, national, regional or local, and find them the perfect way into the heart and heartland of France. As a little bonus, the GR networks are expanding all the time, with the detours — or *varientes* — off the main route eventually linking with other GR paths or *varientes* and becoming GR trails in their own right.

Walkers will find the GR trails generally well marked and easy to follow, and they have two advantages over the footpaths commonly encountered in the UK. First, since they are laid out by local people, they are based on intricate local knowledge of the local sights. If there is a fine view, a mighty castle or a pretty village on your footpath route, your footpath through France will surely lead you to it. Secondly, all French footpaths are usually well provided with a wide range of comfortable country accommodation, and you will discover that the local people, even the farmers, are well used to walkers and greet them with a smile, a '*Bonjour*' and a '*bon route*'.

Terrain and climate

As a glance at these guides or any Topo-guide will indicate, France has a great variety of terrain. France is twice the size of the UK and many natural features are also on a larger scale. There are three main ranges of mountains: the Alps contain the highest mountain in Europe, the Pyrenees go up to 10,000 ft, the Massif Central peaks to over 6000 ft, and there are many similar ranges with hills which overtop our highest British peak, Ben Nevis. On the other hand, the Auvergne and the Jura have marvellous open ridge walking, the Cévennes are steep and rugged, the Ardèche and parts of Provence are hot and wild, the Île de France, Normandy, Brittany and much of Western France is green and pleasant, not given to extremes. There is walking in France for every kind of walker, but given such a choice the wise walker will consider the complications of terrain and weather before setting out, and go suitably equipped.

France enjoys three types of climate: continental, oceanic and mediterranean. South of the Loire it will certainly be hot to very hot from mid-April to late September. Snow can fall on the mountains above 4,000 ft from mid-October and last until May, or even lie year-round on the tops and in couloirs; in the high hills an ice-axe is never a frill. I have used one by the Brêche de Roland in the Pyrenees in mid-June.

Wise walkers should study weather maps and forecasts carefully in the week before they leave' for France, but can generally expect good weather from May to October, and a wide variety of weather — the severity depending on the terrain — from mid-October to the late Spring.

Accommodation

The walker in France can choose from a wide variety of accommodation with the assurance that the walker will always be welcome. This can range from country hotels to wild mountain pitches, but to stay in comfort, many walkers will travel light and overnight in the comfortable hotels of the *Logis de France* network.

Logis de France: The *Logis de France* is a nationwide network of small, family-run country hotels, offering comfortable accommodation and excellent food. *Logis* hotels are graded and can vary from a simple, one-star establishment, with showers and linoleum, to a four- or five-star *logis* with gastronomic menus and deep-pile carpets. All offer excellent value for money, and since there are over 5,000 scattered across the French countryside, they provide a good focus for a walking day. An annual guide to the *Logis* is available from the French Government Tourist Office, 178 Piccadilly, London W1V 0AL, Tel. (01) 491 7622.

Gîtes d'étape: A *gîte d'étape* is best imagined as an unmanned youth hostel for outdoor folk of all ages. They lie all along the footpath networks and are usually signposted or listed in the guides. They can be very comfortable, with bunk beds, showers, a well equipped kitchen, and in some cases they have a warden, a *guardien*, who may offer meals. *Gîtes d'étape* are designed exclusively for walkers, climbers, cyclists, cross country skiers or horse-riders. A typical price (1990) would be Fr.25 for one night. *Gîtes d'étape* should not be confused with a *Gîte de France*. A *gîte* — usually signposted as '*Gîte de France*' — is a country cottage available for a holiday let, though here too, the owner may be more than willing to rent it out as overnight accommodation.

Youth hostels: Curiously enough, there are very few Youth Hostels in France outside the main towns. A full list of the 200 or so available can be obtained from the Youth Hostel Association (YHA), Trevelyan House, St Albans, Herts AL1 2DY.

Pensions or cafes: In the absence of an hotel, a *gîte d'étape* or a youth hostel, all is not lost. France has plenty of accommodation and an enquiry at the village cafe or bar will usually produce a room. The cafe/hotel may have rooms or suggest a nearby pension or a *chambre d'hôte*. Prices start at around Fr.50 for a room, rising to, say, Fr.120. (1990 estimate).

Chambres d'hôte: A *chambre d'hôte* is a guest room or, in English terms, a bed-and-breakfast, usually in a private house. Prices range up from about Fr.60 a night. *Chambres d'hôte* signs are now proliferating in the small villages of France and especially if you can speak a little French are an excellent way to meet the local people. Prices (1990) are from, say, Fr.70 a night for a room, not per person.

Abris: Abris, shelters or mountain huts can be found in the mountain regions, where they are often run by the *Club Alpin Français*, an association for climbers. They range from the comfortable to the primitive, are often crowded and are sometimes reserved for members. Details from the Club Alpin Français, 7 Rue la Boétie, Paris 75008, France.

Camping: French camp sites are graded from one to five star, but are generally very good at every level, although the facilities naturally vary from one cold tap to shops, bars and heated pools. Walkers should not be deterred by a '*Complet*' (Full) sign on the gate or office window: a walker's small tent will usually fit in somewhere. *Camping à la ferme*, or farm camping, is increasingly popular, more primitive — or less regimented — than the official sites, but widely available and perfectly adequate. Wild camping is officially not permitted in National Parks, but unofficially if you are over 1,500m away from a road, one hour's walk from a *gîte* or campsite, and where possible ask permission, you should have no trouble. French country people will always assist the walker to find a pitch.

The law for walkers
The country people of France seem a good deal less concerned about their 'rights' than the average English farmer or landowner. I have never been ordered off land in France or greeted with anything other than friendliness . . . maybe I've been lucky. As a rule, walkers in France are free to roam over all open paths and tracks. No decent walker will leave gates open, trample crops or break down walls, and taking fruit from gardens or orchards is simply stealing. In some parts of France there are local laws about taking chestnuts, mushrooms (and snails), because these are cash crops. Signs like *Réserve de Chasse*, or *Chasse Privé* indicate that the shooting is reserved for the landowner. As a general rule, behave sensibly and you will be tolerated everywhere, even on private land.

The country code
Walkers in France should obey the *Code du Randonneur*:

- Love and respect Nature.
- Avoid unnecessary noise.
- Destroy nothing.
- Do not leave litter.
- Do not pick flowers or plants.
- Do not disturb wildlife.
- Re-close all gates.
- Protect and preserve the habitat.
- No smoking or fires in the forests. (This rule is essential and is actively enforced by foresters and police.)
- Stay on the footpath.
- Respect and understand the country way of life and the country people.
- Think of others as you think of yourself.

Transport
Transportation to and within France is generally excellent. There are no less than nine Channel ports: Dunkirk, Calais, Boulogne, Dieppe, Le Havre, Caen/Ouistreham, Cherbourg, Saint-Malo and Roscoff, and a surprising number of airports served by direct flights from the UK. Although some of the services are seasonal, it is often possible to fly direct to Toulouse, Poitiers, Nantes, Perpignan, Montpellier, indeed to many provincial cities, as well as to Paris and such obvious destinations as Lyon and Nice. Within France the national railway, the SNCF, still retains a nationwide network. Information, tickets and a map can be obtained from the SNCF. France also has a good country bus service and the *gare routière* is often placed just beside the railway station. Be aware though, that many French bus services only operate within the *département*, and they do not generally operate from one provincial city to the next. I cannot encourage people to hitch-hike, which is both illegal and risky, but walkers might consider a taxi for their luggage. Almost every French village has a taxi driver who will happily transport your rucksacks to the next night-stop, fifteen to twenty miles away, for Fr.50 a head or even less.

Money
Walking in France is cheap, but banks are not common in the smaller villages, so carry a certain amount of French money and the rest in traveller's cheques or Eurocheques, which are accepted everywhere.

Clothing and equipment

The amount of clothing and equipment you will need depends on the terrain, the length of the walk, the time of your visit, the accommodation used. Outside the mountain areas it is not necessary to take the full range of camping or backpacking gear. I once walked across France from the Channel to the Camargue along the Grande Randonnée footpaths in March, April and early May and never needed to use any of the camping gear I carried in my rucksack because I found hotels everywhere, even in quite small villages.

Essential items are:

In summer: light boots, a hat, shorts, suncream, lip salve, mosquito repellent, sunglasses, a sweater, a windproof cagoule, a small first-aid kit, a walking stick.
In winter: a change of clothing, stormproof outer garments, gaiters, hat, lip salve, a companion.
In the mountains at any time: large-scale maps (1:25,000), a compass, an ice-axe. In winter, add a companion and ten-point crampons.
At any time: a phrase book, suitable maps, a dictionary, a sense of humour.

The best guide to what to take lies in the likely weather and the terrain. France tends to be informal, so there is no need to carry a jacket or something smart for the evenings. I swear by Rohan clothing, which is light, smart and functional. The three things I would never go without are light, well-broken-in boots and several pairs of loop-stitched socks, and my walking stick.

Health hazards

Health hazards are few. France can be hot in summer, so take a full water-bottle and refill it at every opportunity. A small first-aid kit is sensible, with plasters and 'mole-skin' for blisters, but since prevention is better than cure, loop-stitched socks and flexible boots are better. Any French chemist — a *pharmacie* — is obliged to render first-aid treatment for a small fee. These pharmacies can be found in most villages and large towns and are marked by a green cross.

Dogs are both a nuisance and a hazard. All walkers in France should carry a walking stick to fend off aggressive curs. Rabies — *la rage* — is endemic and anyone bitten must seek immediate medical advice. France also possesses two types of viper, which are common in the hill areas of the south. In fairness, although I found my walking stick indispensable, I must add that in thirty years I have never even seen a snake or a rabid dog. In case of real difficulty, dial 17 for the police and the ambulance.

Food and wine

One of the great advantages with walking in France is that you can end the day with a good meal and not gain an ounce. French country cooking is generally excellent and good value for money, with the price of a four-course menu starting at about Fr.45. The ingredients for the mid-day picnic can be purchased from the village shops and these also sell wine. Camping-Gaz cylinders and cartridges are widely available, as is 2-star petrol for stoves. Avoid naked fires.

Preparation

The secret of a good walk lies in making adequate preparations before you set out. It pays to be fit enough to do the daily distance at the start. Much of the necessary information is contained in this guide, but if you need more, look in guidebooks or outdoor magazines, or ask friends.

The French

I cannot close this introduction without saying a few words about the French, not least because the walker in France is going to meet rather more French people than, say, a motorist will, and may even meet French people who have never met a foreigner before. It does help if the visitor speaks a little French, even if only enough to say '*bonjour*' and '*Merci*' and '*S'il vous plaît*'. The French tend to be formal and it pays to be polite, to say 'hello', to shake hands. I am well aware that relations between France and England have not always been cordial over the last six hundred years or so, but I have never met with hostility of any kind in thirty years of walking through France. Indeed, I have always found that if the visitor is prepared to meet the French halfway, they will come more than halfway to greet him or her in return, and are both friendly and hospitable to the passing stranger.

As a final tip, try smiling. Even in France, or especially in France, a smile and a '*pouvez vous m'aider?*' (Can you help me?) will work wonders. That's my last bit of advice, and all I need do now is wish you '*Bonne Route*' and good walking in France.

THE DORDOGNE

It is hard to imagine a part of France more spectacularly attractive than the Dordogne. Once known as the province of Périgord, it is an area of great natural beauty, harmony and infinite variety. From the granite formations around Nontron to the vineyards of Bergerac, or from the forest and tarns of La Double to the deeply sculpted limestone valleys of the Sarlat district, fresh vistas unfold all the time. Summer or winter, the traveller will never tire of the beauty of its ever-changing scenery.

The Dordogne lies between the foothills of the Massif Central and the plains of Guyenne. It slopes east to west and north-east to south-west. The principal rivers, the Lizonne, the Dronne, the Beauronne, the Isle, the Auvézère, spread out like a fan. Many of these begin as great torrents before calming down to converge and flow in to the majestic River Dordogne, one of the longest in France.

A marvellous area

The Dordogne has such a rich variety of landscapes and such diverse natural resources that to choose just a few walking tours from all those that could be made along the ancient footpaths is an almost impossible task. The multitude of pathways, many of them thousands of years old, the waterways and little roads forgotten in the mists of time, make it a paradise for walking.

The soil in the Dordogne is derived mainly from the Mesozoic limestone plateaux bounded in the north-east by the Palaeozoic rocks of the last foothills of the Massif Central and, in the south-west, by the Tertiary sands of the Aquitanian basin. Powerful rivers cut across the Cretaceous formations, shaping a wild but unpretentious landscape and bringing a large part of the area under the influence of the soft Atlantic climate. Oak and chestnut trees form a cool dark shroud across the hills, intersected by hollows filled with underbrush and shimmering lines of poplars. Rust-coloured cliffs and strangely-shaped rocks abound. Châteaux and stone-roofed cottages stand at the end of drives lined with walnut trees. The area has a unique charm and the walker is the first to realize that however interesting the National Museum of Prehistory and the famous caverns and rock shelters, there is nothing to beat wandering free along the ancient footpaths, searching for Cro-Magnon ancestors among the juniper-clad cliffs and damp hollows, or on the rocky sun-warmed terraces.

The Dordogne is indisputably a treasury of natural beauty, prehistory, art, architecture and traditional hospitality. So put on your walking shoes and set off to sample its delights for yourself. You will be stunned by the physical beauty of the area, the rolling wooded hills, known as pechs, barren limestone plateaux (Causses), lush and fertile valleys, walnut trees in all their glory, huge chestnuts and oaks, stately poplars, vineyards. And between the walks enjoy the provincial cuisine — the Dordogne is one of the best known culinary areas of France — the friendly warm-hearted hospitality, the peace and quiet, the golden châteaux, the churches, regional architecture and prehistoric caves and art.

Prehistoric Périgord

As well as being famous for its beautiful landscape, and architectural interest, Dordogne is known as the 'capital of prehistory'. And, despite conservation problems and the fact that most of the prehistoric works of art are now in major national and international museums, there are still many natural sites to delight the eye and gladden the soul.

The National Museum of Prehistory at Les Eyzies, together with museums at Périgord and Brive, house one of the most important collections of stone and bone exhibits in the world. The Périgord region has witnessed a succession of civilizations, ranging from the Homo Faber, represented by the Mousterian and Ferrassian cultures in particular, to Homo Sapiens including the Chancelade culture, Cro-Magnon man and Combe-Capelle man.

Throughout the region are caves, rock shelters and stratified evidence of prehistoric human habitation. Each of these civilizations has left truly remarkable traces of its existence throughout the region. The rise of the Aurignacian culture saw the emergence of works of art, which reached a high point of realism and beauty during the flowering of the Magdalenian culture.

Visitors cannot fail to wonder about the activities of the successive civilizations which inhabited the territory of the Dordogne, and feel inspired to know more. As you walk along a rocky track overlooking a bend in the valley, or stand at the bottom of a hollow examining the stratigraphic section of a prehistoric rock-shelter, you come face to face with the power of human inspiration, and begin to understand how man's gradually expanding intelligence was able to raise humanity above the animals, giving him the ability to appreciate life in all its fullness and glory.

No one is sure why paintings, carvings and sculptures were created in the barely accessible depths of subterranean caverns, but it is certainly possible that they express the deer hunters' religious devotion to the giver of life and death. The prehistoric artists had wonderful powers of observation and were supremely skilled at using the simplest means (flint tools, charcoal sticks or powdered mineral oxide) to depict realistic scenes of everyday fauna which shared their waterholes and hunting grounds. The meaning of some of these symbols is lost to us, but many believe that they are proof of a highly developed spirituality among peoples who, on occasions, raised their art to the highest standards of beauty.

Churches and châteaux

When you cross the River Dordogne, the fifth largest river in France, or walk among the hillsides of the River Lot, you cannot fail to notice the powerful struggles that have taken place over the centuries in this part of France. Imposing fortified châteaux oppose one another across the River Dordogne which served as a fortification line while wars dragged on interminably in earlier times.

During the troubled period from 1216 to 1337, which has been called the first hundred years war (as distinct from the Hundred Years War, which started in 1337) at least 1,000 fortified châteaux were built on rocky heights and dominated strategic positions on roads and rivers. Only a handful now remain in Dordogne and these were enlarged or rebuilt later. The fortified stronghold of Monpazier was constructed at the end of the 13th century for Edward I of England. The town was to change hands between the French and English many times before the turbulent period of war came to an end. Traces of the town's rectangular ground plan can still be seen. Monpazier has old houses separated by narrow back streets, a church, and a central covered market with grain measures and overhanging eaves.

The château de Biron stands on high ground, dominating the countryside for 30 kilometres, and was once the most important baronial seat in the region. Its buildings, dating from the 12th to 17th centuries, are inextricably intertwined and vividly evoke the severity of sieges and reparations to which they were subjected.

Everywhere in the region you will come across Romanesque churches. The ninth century saw relative peace and prosperity in church and State, and gave birth to a great resurgence of religious foundations. From about the late 10th to 13th centuries, over 1,000 churches, abbeys, and priories were built in the Dordogne. Some were large, others small, many are dilapidated, some have been restored; but nearly every commune today has some monument to the Romanesque style of architecture.

The strongholds of Périgord

Strongholds, or fortified towns, are mainly to be found in the Midi (Southern France), and are most common in Périgord, which was once a border separating the possessions of the kings of England, who also held the title Duke of Aquitaine, and the territories ruled from Paris by the kings of France. There are 25 such strongholds in Périgord and a certain number in the Agen, Bordeaux and Quercy regions. The nearest one to be found anywhere further north is in Champagne.

Strongholds date from the first Hundred Years War, and were constructed during a curiously short period of no more than 50 years. The oldest in the region was built at Villefranche-du-Périgord on the orders of Alphonse de Poitiers, brother to French king Saint-Louis, in 1259. Then in 1270, Edward I of England founded Lalinde, Beaumont-du-Périgord, Molière and finally Monpazier. The English and French faced one another from these fortified emplacements and, from the military point of view, effectively cancelled out each other's strongholds.

The problem of where to build was solved by convincing a monastic order or feudal lord that it would be in everyone's best interest if land was cheerfully donated. The King's agent would then sink a post at the spot chosen for the centre of the main square (or, sometimes, rectangle) and from there, main streets 8 metres wide and other streets 6 metres wide were marked out at right angles with measuring line, giving a grid layout inside a walled enclosure. This was itself square or rectangular, and pierced with gates at the 4 cardinal points.

Sites were then set aside for a fortified church, town hall and covered market, after which the remaining building space was allocated freely between interested parties in equal sized plots 8 metres wide (being the span of a beam made from a single tree). Prospective citizens were attracted by promises of lower taxes or even total freedom from feudal dues, which is why Villefranche (Free Town) crops up so often in place names.

Newcomers had to promise, on pain of a fine, to build in a certain way and within a well-defined time limit, and also to share in collective works such as construction of the church and the enclosure walls. Those who were granted plots around the main square undertook to set their ground floors back behind arches and pillars, giving a wide covered pavement which was cool in summer and sheltered in winter for strolling round the shops. This style of building is referred to as cornières (overhanging eaves). At times the king grew impatient if these time limits were not met. In 1289 Edward I issued a date for final completion of Monpazier with penalties for failure to comply.

Today as we walk through the streets and squares of these strongholds, so miraculously preserved, it is as if time has stood still. In the past, behind these walls people endured sieges, surviving for months until peace returned, thanks to the grain and bacon stored in the Consular Granaries.

The stone-built houses were comfortable. To the rear, the dwelling led onto a minor street or back alleyway called an andronne. Some houses were separated from the one next door by a narrow corridor which held rainwater. This gave excellent protection against fire, and all common ownership rights were waived.

There were stores and workshops for every trade, from the barber, the weaver and the tanner to the butcher and the baker. The market was held each week, on a particular day laid down by royal decree, ensuring that trade prospered, and there were two or three fairs every year to which customers and merchants came from far and wide, attracted by the freedom of the town. These vast gatherings were the occasion for festivals or pilgrimages, or for asserting respect for the hand of authority by carrying out executions. In the main square at Monpazier, on 6 August 1637, one of the leaders of the Peasants' Revolt, a weaver named Buffarot, was broken on the rack and his body quartered. His remains were then displayed around the neighbouring parishes as grim warnings. On the other hand, the most extraordinary pomp was lavished on visiting princes and rulers, to the great delight of the crowds.

As peace and prosperity grew throughout the land, the walled strongholds, such as Domme, perched upon their crags, and therefore difficult to reach, no longer held such an attraction for the populace. Trade and craftsmanship declined in the fortified towns, and their populations dwindled. Today they look like magnificent film sets.

From an article in MAIF informations, June 1977.

The Gorges de l'Aveyron

The region is bursting with architectural interest and scenic wonders. It has a variety of touring centres and vast amounts of open space, making it the ideal choice for the walker, as well as the cyclist, canoeist, horserider and potholer. Many villages and local associations have shown great initiative in waymarking nearly 600 kilometres of footpaths for the long-distance walker, and these are backed up by a network of gîtes d'étape to provide overnight accommodation.

The peaceful footpaths give easy access to the natural attractions of the area and provide meeting places for walkers to exchange and compare impressions. The footpaths are administered by four départmements: Aveyron, Lot, Tarn and Tarn-et-Garonne.

The rivers Aveyron and Viaur, which converge at Laguépie, form the backbone of the region. The climate is mild and sunny (annual rainfall 700 to 800mm) and the sun shines for between 2,000 to 2,500 hours a year.

There are three sub-divisions in the region:

1. *The south-western edge of the Ségala of Rouergue.* The Palaeozoic plateau of Ségala (height 804 metres at Rieupeyroux) ends above the Aveyron valley (250 to 150 metres). This plateau (once heathland, chestnut groves and barley crops — wheat had to be fetched from the Causse area) has been undergoing a revolution in agriculture since the turn of the century and is now very productive, concentrating on cattle, pigs, wheat, maize and potatoes.

During the same period the valley between Villefranche and Laguépie was in economic decline because the hillslope vineyards had been destroyed by the phylloxera outbreak which began in 1875, and the harvest from the chestnut plantations was very poor. As a result, farming underwent widespread development.

Industry in this part of the region is unobtrusive: meat-packing and nuts and bolts (Villefranche); shoes (Laguépie); the quarries are more obvious, especialy the Lexos cement works.

As far as tourism is concerned, Najac has become an undisputed centre of attraction; Villefranche-de-Rouergue is the main focus of regional activity, a centre for business, schools and hospitals; and the town of Laguépie is well known for business and tourism.

2. The Quercy-Rouergue border. Between Parisot and Saint-Antonin, where the Mesozoic formations of Quercy and the Palaeozoic formations of Rouergue meet, cuestas rise above an undulating plateau and the tranquil valleys of the rivers Bonnette, Seye and Baye. The land used to be given over to wheat, but this has now made way for mixed arable farming and cattle and sheep.

The southern part is a projection from the Causses in Quercy, cut by the Aveyron gorge, riddled with caverns, covered with forests and interspersed with picturesque sites (Saint-Antonin, Penne, Briniquel). The old industries — tanneries and textiles at Saint-Antonin; foundaries at Bruniquel; straw plaiting for the hat trade at Caylus — are now only a memory. Once Saint-Antonin and Feneyrols even had thermal spas. Tourism in this area is increasing, despite limited facilities. Substantial investment is, however, planned: small hotels; farm camping sites; guest houses, and country gîtes.

3. The north-western Causses of the Tarn. Limestone plateaux rise up from the Cérou valley, where mixed arable farming is common, as it is in the valley of the Vère, overlooked to the south by ridges and to the north by La Grésigne forest. The latter is situated in a vast depression which has been carved in a Permian dome — at the summit of this stands Vaour. La Grésigne, which is a well-kept State forest of 4,000 hectares, where wild boar and deer are free to roam as they please among groves and coppices of oak, is managed by the Office National des Forêts (French National Forestry Commission).

Tourists come to look at reminders of the past in the elevated old towns of Cordes, Castelnau-de-Montmiral, Puycelci and Salvagnac, and to savour the wines of the region which, between Cordes and Cahuzac, forms the northern part of the Gaillac wine district.

Pilgram halts

Religion, pilgrims and pilgrimages have always played a large part in the life, art, architecture and landscape of the Périgord region. Over the centuries pilgrims converged on the Pyrénées from north, north-east and east, venerating the relics of saints at the sanctuaries along the way.

Known pilgrims are not numerous. Along the Le Puy route, for example, only two halts have been identified with any certainty. These are the basilica of Sainte-Foy at Conques and the abbey of Saint Peter at Moissac. Rouergue is almost certainly the province most closely associated with the Road of St James — one of the first recorded pilgrims was Count Raymond II of Rouergue, killed in Spain by the Saracens in 961 whilst negotiating the Cantabrian coast.

In recent times the Centre for Compostellan Studies has set out to identify the main, secondary and lateral pilgrim routes. These have been drawn up on the basis of the hospitals known to have acted as refuges and stopping places, as well as the abbeys and priories of religious orders which gave protection and shelter to travellers and pilgrims. By studying 16th, 17th and 18th-century maps, and the Table drawn up by Peutinger giving a broad outline of the Roman road network, it has been possible to gain a fairly precise view of the lines of communication open in the Middle Ages.

Manuscripts relating to the travels of important people have also yielded valuable information.

Among the great sanctuaries of the Middle Ages, Rocamadour was 'the most popular in Europe in 1218' and also welcomed pilgrims travelling to Santiago de Compostella and Rome. What is now the region of the Lot was once criss-crossed with pilgrim routes. For example, there were six routes from Notre-Dame de Rocamadour — one went to Santiago de Compostella and two went to Rome.

The routes which we do know about date mostly from the 18th century. Pilgrimages are often associated with old cobbled trackways flanked with stone walls (Gaulish tracks, Roman roads and so on). Along such trails are found refreshing springs, and mounds of stones sometimes surmounted by a cross. These cairns are known as montjoys, and showed the way to the crossroads. Each pilgrim, on foot, would stop at the cairn, pray and add his stone to the pile.

Where the paths forded or, more rarely, bridged a river, or if they passed through a region which was deserted or frequented by bandits, fortified houses and hospices were built.

Glossary of Archaeology

Archaeological dig: Technique for uncovering the various layers or relics of archaeological interest on an ancient site.

Aurignacian: Upper Palaeolithic industry contemporary with the emergence of Cro-Magnon man (between 30,000 and 27,000 years BC); named after deposits discovered at Aurignac (Haute-Garonne).

Chatelperronian: Upper Palaeolithic (or Lower Périgordian) industry dating from the start of the latter period between 35,000 and 30,000 years BC, possibly coinciding with Combe-Capelle man; takes its name from deposits at Chatel-Perron (Allier).

Glaciation: A period during which the earth's climate cooled and the surface area of the ice caps increased. The main glacial periods were: Günz (650,000 to 500,000 years BC), Mindel (400,000 to 320,000 years BC), Riss (200,000 to 120,000 years BC) and Würm (75,000 to 10,000 years BC).

Gravettian: Upper Palaeolithic (or Upper Périgordian) industry dating from the period between 27,000 and 20,000 years BC; named after finds of deposits at La Gravette (Bayac).

Magdalenian: Upper Palaeolithic industry dating from between 17,000 and 10,000 years BC; named after deposits at La Madeleine (Tursac). The wet and temperate interstadial period of Lascaux occurred around the 15th millenium BC.

Mesolithic: (Middle Stone Age) Period of transition between the Upper Palaeolithic and the Neolithic periods, making its appearance about 10,000 years BC in certain regions.

Micoquian: Middle Palaeolithic industry dating from between 120,000 and 70,000 years BC, contemporary with the Mousterian; named after finds at La Micoque (Les Eyzies).

Mousterian: Middle Palaeolithic industry associated with Neanderthal man, between 100,000 and 35,000 BC; takes its name from deposits found at Le Moustier (Peyzac).

Neolithic: (New Stone Age) The age of polished stone implements, arising in certain regions about 8,000 years BC.

Palaeolithic: (Old Stone Age) The age of the flaked stone tool, dating back as much as one million years and lasting until around 10,000 BC. Homo Sapiens appeared during the Upper Palaeolithic about 35,000 BC.

Périgordian: Series of Upper Palaeolithic industries placed between the Mousterian and the Solutrean which, according to certain French scholars such as Peyrony, existed alongside the Aurignacian industry. Lower Périgordian is known as Chatelperronian and Upper Périgordian is called Gravettian.

Prehistoric art: Sometimes called 'cave art'. The terms refer to works of art from a period in the history of mankind for which there are no clear written records. The development of prehistoric art occurred during the Upper Palaeolithic period, contemporary with the emergence of the Aurignacian industry.

Rock-shelter: A hollow beneath an overhanging rock-face, used by man and animals as protection from the elements. Accumulated debris on its floor can reveal bones left over from feeding, discarded stone flakes, blunt flint tools, items lost or left behind during a hasty retreat and the remains of fires, interspersed with layers of fallen earth or rubble from the sides and roof of the shelter or from the cliff-face. In some rock-shelters, successive layers of archaeological material may be separated by a thick band yielding no remains of interest, indicating that the shelter was unoccupied for a long period, or that there had been a serious rock-fall.

Solutrean: Upper Palaeolithic industry dating from between 20,000 and 15,000 BC; named after the deposits discovered at Solutré (Saône-et-Loire).

Tayacian: Term applied to certain levels of the industries discovered at La Micoque (Tayac-les-Eyzies).

Tectiforms: Roof-shaped symbols. May be seen at La Mouthe, Font de Gaume and Bernifal in particular.

Some regional terms

The following are expressions in the Langue d'Oc (also known as Occitan):

Barry, or Embarry: suburb of a town.

Bolet: refers to a particular part of a rural house in Quercy. It is a roofed-in reception terrace leading to the main living room.

Cabécou: name of a range of very small goat cheeses.

Calade: paved street or track.

Caminol: diminutive of cami, a small path.

Cayrou — borie — caselle (or cazelle) — gariotte (or garriotte): these terms are found in regions where the ground is very stony, where the peasant had to clear his land of rocks before he could sow his crops. As a result, he built up 'cayrous', heaps of stones, from which to build walls or 'capitelles' according to his needs. 'Capitelle' is the general term used to describe the humble dry-stone structure found everywhere on the Causse. Sometimes called borie, caselle or gariotte, they are evidence of old pastoral cultures. Some of these dry-stone shelters were occupied by shepherds and winegrowers until fairly recently.

Clédo: wooden or iron trellis used as a movable enclosure.

Combe: small dry valley or hollow partly filled with falls of 'grèze' (stony soil — see below). The floor of the hollow is generally covered in red soil.

Conques: small valley, hollow.

Courderc (le): garden or meadow, generally closed, next to a farm.

Coyau: (also 'coiel', 'coiaux' or 'coe') equivalent of the French word 'queue' meaning 'tail'. This represents the small piece of wood which extends a rafter beyond the outside of the wall.

Fonteille: possibly a corruption of 'Fonteta' — little spring.

Fromental: wheat field.

Grèze: stony soil found as a deposit on hillsides, consisting of small argillo-calcareous pebbles bound in an argillaceous matrix. After trying unsuccessfully to cultivate this mean soil, farmers now tend to leave it fallow.

Igue: circular pit; swallow hole. Feature of limestone (karst) regions. The Causse is a typically fissured limestone region, and therefore very permeable. Percolating rainwater dissolves the rock and forms cavities. The 'igue' sometimes leads to caverns or galleries which no longer carry running water. The network of chambers is, therefore, dry, but in most cases the active river can be found some hundred metres or so below. An 'igue' may be from 20 to 100 or more metres deep.
Lauzes: sheets of quarry stone a few centimetres thick.
Montredon: rounded mountain.
Pech: the occitan form of the French word 'puy' meaning 'hill' (often, as it happens, volcanic in origin).
Soleilho: an open-sided loft. It was the upper floor of a dwelling, used for storing provisions and anything which needed drying.

Specialities of the area

Meals in the Dordogne are very special! Périgord is not just a place for eating well — the region is famous for its superb cuisine, and its culinary skills are regarded as a fine art. There is nothing exotic about the ingredients, though. They can be found in any rural home. Every farmer's wife fattens her own geese for foie-gras. Every smallholder keeps poultry and pigs for galantine of turkey or hand of pork. And truffles, though sadly now becoming scarce, can be found beneath oak-trees known as 'truffiers'.

A meal worthy of its place of origin must be savoured with respect. In Périgord, cuisine is not a subject to be taken lightly. Around here, the most popular seasoning with any meal is conversation. And they certainly know how to tell a good story in these parts. This ancient land is imbued with ancient legends and has produced some gifted writers: Montaigne, Brantôme, Fénelon, Joubert. Stay to savour the meals and table-talk, and you will meet artists who are proud to be experts in both. Remember, of the many superb products of the Dordogne, the finest are its men and women.
ANDRÉ MAUROIS
Member of the Académie Française

Foie gras

Foie gras is handed down to us from the geese of Ancient Gaul and the figs of Ancient Rome. This is no fantasy, but a tiny historical fact with which you can amaze your friends. Indeed, those huge flocks of Gaulish geese which Gaston Bonheur showed swarming towards Italy in *Notre patrie gauloise* (Our Gaulish Heritage) were not going there simply to guard the Capitol. They were also on their way for fattening, so that the followers of Lucullus could enjoy goose liver as a delicacy.

In Latin the word for liver was *jecur*. The best livers were from geese fattened on figs or, in Latin, *ficatum*. Foie gras was called in Latin *jecur ficatum*, which was then shortened by leaving out the first word. In France, the Latin word *ficatum* eventually became *foie*, which is now the everyday word for liver!

But we should remember that the goose, once described as *a foie gras factory on legs*, existed before Gaul and Ancient Rome. It was the first bird ever to be domesticated. Well before the cock had crowed thrice, the tomb of Princess Atet was decorated with frescoes showing that the Ancient Egyptians (and probably the Persians and the Assyrians before them) knew about keeping geese. Another tomb, near Memphis, even has bas-reliefs which prove that they knew about force-feeding.

When we consider the *Goose Child* by Boethos of Chalcedon, or the dream of Penelope in which she likened her suitors to the geese in the palace courtyard, and in the light of Cato's *De Re Rustica*, or the banquet of Nasidienus, where Horace describes 'boys bearing a vast dish garnished with joints of male crane, liver of white hen-goose sumptuously fattened on figs, shoulders of hare and grilled breast of thrushes', we find that geese play a lesser part on the gourmet's table than the enlargement of the liver might lead us to believe.

Gaul was the land of geese. Here they have remained supreme, in Alsace, in Périgord and in the South-west, where it became first a sacred duty and then a way of life to fatten geese. Later on, ducks were fattened in the same way.

ROBERT J. COURTINE
From an article in TOURING magazine, October 1979.

The Vine arbour

The scenery in the Lot wine-growing region is divided up by rows of vines which intersect with geometric precision. Yet vines used to be trained in many different ways, some of which have been in use since the begining of time. Although these ways have largely disappeared, we still find situations where vines are trained upwards, for the purpose of growing dessert grapes. Vine stocks still trained in this way are generally found close to the house, on large wooden pergolas or trellises along the façade of a building.

The shape into which the vine is trained depends on the variety of grape and pruning method. If there is a risk of frost, vines may be raised on arbours, as we find in the Lacapelle-Marival region or the north of the region. But it is also safe to assume that arbours are erected outside houses in the Lot region because they are attractive. They play an important climatic role by providing cool shade in summer and letting the sun shine through onto the walls of the house in winter.

Because they have such a variety of shapes, arbours are one of the most attractive ways of extending the lines of a house. They are a transition between interior and exterior, an interplay of the artificial and the growing, all of which explains their versatile charm.

The structure itself is generally of iron, and is used to produce a variety of shapes, from the simple arch to decorative scrolls.

FROM LAURENCE TOULET, Architect.
From the booklet *Vigne et vin, culte et culture* (Vine and Wine, the Cult and the Crop) published by *Conservation des Antiquités et Objets d'art du Lot* (Lot Antiquities and Art Preservation Trust).

Cahors wine

It is impossible to say precisely when vines were first introduced into Quercy. They certainly existed during the Roman occupation. Around AD96 a Roman emperor had vines uprooted and replaced with corn, in an attempt to repress any competition with wines from the Italian peninsula. Then about AD275, replanting was allowed, and the inhabitants of Quercy sent to Italy for the best varieties, particularly the Amminaea, still grown to this day under the name Auxerrois pied de perdrix (Auxerrois partridge foot).

The vineyards of Cahors extend south of Quercy, from the little village of Accambal, upstream of Cahors, to the Lot-et-Garonne boundary, in a strip 100 kilometres wide extending along both banks of the River Lot.

Vines are grown on the flat in the plains of the River Lot, as well as on hillside terraces and, as in days gone by, on the shoulders of the great limestone plateau called the Causse. Today there are 1,000 hectares of vine producing 45,000 to 50,000 hectolitres of Cahors wine.

WALK 1

ANGOULÊME

🏠 ✕ 🚂 🚌 🚃

The city is built on a promontory and is surrounded by ramparts which form a promenade. Of the château constructed for Isabelle d'Angoulême, who was Queen of England by marriage to King John (nicknamed Lackland because he had no land!) only two towers remain. These are now part of the Hôtel de Ville (Town Hall). It is thought that Marguerite de Valois, sister of French king François I, was born and brought up in one of these towers. The cathedral is the jewel of the city, a lovely 12th century Romanesque building with alterations. It is noted for its domes and its remarkable exterior sculptures.

The walk begins in Puymoyen, a village on the south of Angoulême. The bus for Puymoyen leaves from the Place du Champs de Mars hourly except Sundays.

PUYMOYEN

🏠 ✕ 🍷 🚌

The Auberge des Roches keeps the keys for the CAF (Club Alpin Français) refuge known as Eaux Claires. This accommodates 15 people, but has no water supply.

1Km
0:15

From the car park in front of the mairie, GR36 follows the D104 road which leads south-east; after 100 metres take the path which heads south out of a little square on the right immediately beyond the church. This leads to the Charse road. Go south on this and you will come to the CAF refuge, Eaux Claires.

Refuge Eaux Claires

🏠

Follow the road until a little farther on you reach a fork.

Detour, *10 mins*
Vallon des Eaux Claires
At the fork take the right-hand path (GR4 on the map)

To continue with GR36, take the left hand road, cross the Eaux Claires stream and make for the Petit Chamoulard farm. Behind the farm, on the left, is a cave called the Grotte des Faux-

heading north-west. You can visit Le Verger paper-mill where paper is made by hand; look for prehistoric deposits or climb rocks.

5Km
1:15

Andole

7Km
1:45

FOUQUEBRUNE
Y ⚖

5Km
1:20

Monnayeurs. After another 500 metres, take a track which rejoins the road. Follow the road as far as the hamlet of Charse.

Keep Charse on your right and go left (east) on a stony track leading to the woods. After 200 metres you come to a fork. Take the right-hand side (pond on the left). When this paved woodland trail reaches the D41 road, turn left (east). After 600 metres, near a wash house, turn right onto a path which crosses the valley and then follow it towards the south-east. On reaching a road, follow it left (east) to the little village called Andole.

On reaching the first few houses turn right, then right again a little further on. Take the dirt track leading in a southerly direction — there are walled fields on either side at first — and on reaching the D43 road head immediately east along a paved path. You pass La Faye on the left and come out onto the D101 road. Turn right onto it, but then go almost immediately left in a southerly direction following the boundary between the two fields for a distance of 500 metres. Within site of the houses of Chez Godet where there is a pedestal of a broken wayside cross turn left (east) towards the sheep-pens at La Côte. Then take a tarmac road which skirts Chez Jamet and leads to the D122 road. Turn right onto this road and stay on it until the village of Fouquebrune.

Go past the church and take the D43 road towards the south-east. After the wayside cross, go left (east) onto a little road which goes on to skirt south of Goulée. Cross the D81 road and keep going for another 600 metres. Turn left onto a pathway into the woods. On leaving the woods turn sharp right and then left, skirting north of Le Puy de Courolle. You will go through more woods and will probably find that some of the waymarkers have been damaged or destroyed. After a short while you will come to the hamlet of Tournesou.

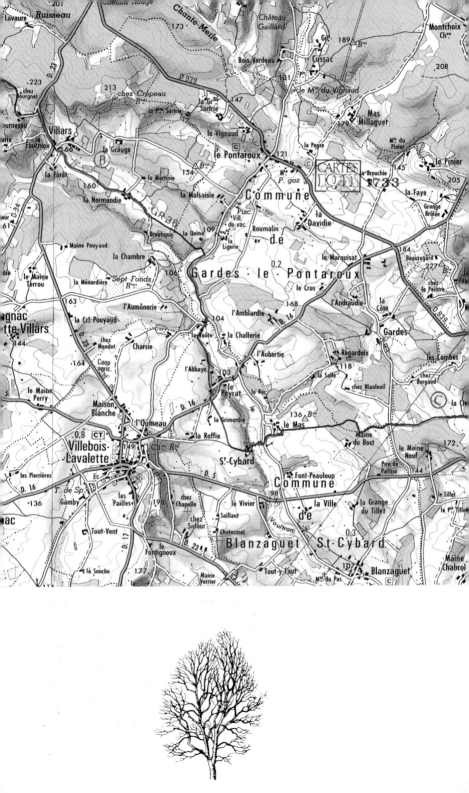

Tournesou

This is a picturesque little village which has been used as a film set.

3Km
0:45

La Quina

Renowned for its series of prehistoric deposits excavated by Dr. Henri Martin. There is an enormous rock, known as the 'Mushroom', which, at some time in the past, broke loose from the cliff by erosion.

3Km
0:45

Detour, *15 mins*
LE PONTAROUX

Turn left (north) to Le Pontaroux.

Tarmac road
Detour, *20 mins*
VILLEBOIS-LAVALETTE

Take the tarmac road towards the west.

4Km
1:00

Follow the road eastwards, then take a path leading to the D23, turning right (south) onto this road. Keeping Villars hamlet on your left, continue along a narrow road to La Normandie. Some 500 metres beyond the farms, leave the road and keep straight ahead on a path dropping down towards the valley of the Voultron. You will reach the Blanzaguet to Le Pontaroux road at a little place called La Quina.

To continue with GR36, turn right (south) along the road. At a small place called La Voûte there is a fork. Turn right, cross the stream and then go left along a dirt track which follows the right bank of the Voultron as far as Le Peyrat, where you pass to the right of the houses. The footpath comes out onto the D16 road. Cross the road, and follow a paved path straight ahead. Some 750 metres farther on, you come to a tarmac road joining the little villages of La Roffie and Saint-Cybard.

To continue with the GR36, turn left onto the tarmac road, to St. Cybard. Cross the bridge over the Voultron, and then the road. Continue until the path leads up the steps of a wayside cross where there is a narrow road used by the farms at Le Mas. Turn left onto this road and keep to the right of the farms. Head east following a dirt path which eventually crosses a wood, and then continues as a paved road, until it intersects with a road. A minor footpath (PR) with yellow waymarkers leads to the Pontaroux camping site, a walk of about 1 hour 30 minutes. Keep heading east towards the village of Édon.

ÉDON
♆

2Km
0:30

Go along by the church. At the crossroads, where there is a statue of the Virgin Mary, take the tarmac path which drops down to the road. Cross the road and continue ahead along a pathway leading to the D199 road. Turn right onto the D199 to La Rochebeaucourt-et-Argentine.

LA ROCHEBEAUCOUT-ET-ARGENTINE
🏠 ✕ ♆ ⚓ 🚌

The original 15th century château of La Rochebeaucourt was burned down in 1943. The magnificent Gout plain was a vineyard of distinction until the vine disease, phylloxera, put an end to it a century ago. Cereal crops are now grown instead of vines. When you reach L'Echandeuil you can see on the hillside about 3 km away, the village of Gout-Rossignol with its square belfry. In very clear weather it is possible to see Bertric-Burée and Le Puy de Beaumont, on the horizon 20 km to the south (Ribérac region and Dronne valley).

8.5Km
2:20

Walk through the town and leave by the Ribérac road (south). Some 200 metres beyond the last houses, go left along the path to Argentine, then head south-east and skirt the airfield on the plateau. The paving slabs beside the footpath formed the Roman road from Périgueux to Saintes. Keep going and cross the disused railway bridge. Walk along the track in a south-easterly direction for about 1,800 metres. On reaching the former level-crossing at La Durantie, turn right onto the road and follow it to L'Echandeuil. From here the Gout-Rossignol plain starts to come into view.

Continue along the road from L'Echandeuil. At the road junction, cross over and go straight on. In a short time you will pass, on your left, the private driveway of the Château de Beaulieu. Cross the N708 and take the paved country pathway straight ahead of you, which leads to the little village of Beauclaveau. As you leave the hamlet turn left onto a road for just 30 metres. At the intersection, (where there is an electricity transformer) take the path to the left (north-east) to Château de Beauregard.

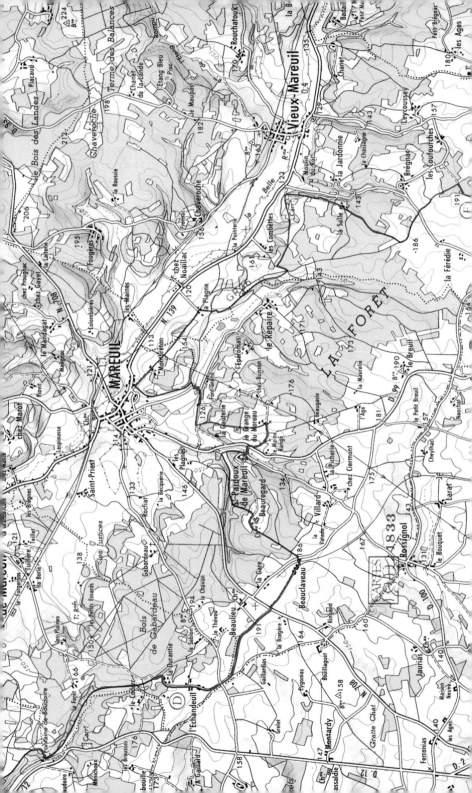

Château de Beauregard

This country seat dates from the 13th, 16th and 17th centuries. It is not open to visitors.

4Km
1:10

MAREUIL

✗ ⚘ ⚒ ▬ 🛈

A former baronial seat of Périgord

4Km
1

Go around the outside of the garden in front of the château, then down the path, and left into the woods. The path runs along a small, grassy valley for some 500 metres. At some large, overhanging rocks, cross the valley on the right and go up the other side through the trees to the square-towered Romanesque church at Saint-Pardoux-de-Mareuil. Leave Saint-Pardoux by the tarmac pathway, continue to the bottom of the main valley and cross the stream. Then cross the D99, go slightly right and follow the path upwards on the opposite side of the road.

When you reach the piece of high ground in the hamlet of La Grange-du-Moreau, turn left between the houses, follow the country pathway between the plots of land and then continue straight on through the woods. At the foot of the slope, turn right onto a paved track and follow it until it intersects with the road from Mareuil to Le Repaire. Turn left (this was formerly a peat moor) and, after another 100 metres, take a dirt track towards the rocks. Go on for about 80 metres and take another dirt path going upwards to the left. This brings you out above the La-Croix-des-Martres building development overlooking Mareuil village.

The GR36 turns right (south-east) onto a track up to Montbreton farm. Take the grassy track in front of Montbreton farm and continue straight across open country to Les Plagnes farm. On reaching the first of the buildings turn right, cross the farmyard and head south-east towards a rocky ridge between the fields, on the edge of the heath. Follow this rocky ridge above the valley of the Prés-Sauvages, there is a former peat bog at the bottom. The route of the path is sketchily waymarked in places. Not much further on, the path leads out onto a paved track coming up from the valley floor. Follow this to the left. Come back to a south-easterly direction by bearing right along the main trail. Keep going straight ahead over the heath and between the junipers. Walk along side a walled field, climbing slightly upwards, then turn left at the end of the field onto a path which drops down towards Les Combettes farm. After some 50 metres, take the first dirt

Corniche de la Belle

A ridge overlooking the Belle valley with views of the Château de Chaveroche.

Detour, *15 mins*

VIEUX-MAREUIL

𝒴 ✕ ⚓ 🚌

6Km
1:30

LEGUILLAC-DE-CERCLES

𝒴 ⚓

Romanesque church with a handsome steeple and two domes above the nave.

5Km
1:15

La Verrerie

Some of the houses are interesting, built in the Quercy style, with a terrace or staircase below an overhanging storey.

path on the right towards a wooded heath. Leave this path and turn east across a poorly waymarked footpath crossing the heath. After another kilometre, you will come to Corniche de la Belle.

Detour see left. Walk down the N139 road and follow it (east) to the right.

The GR continues south again up a rocky ridge (quarries nearby) and comes out onto the paved track to La Salle. Turn right still heading south. Beyond the houses, go between some hedges onto a country pathway, still heading south, through some woods, across heathland and then along some enclosed fields. The path then bends south-east and comes out onto the narrow road from Brégnac to La Férédie. Cross this road. The next part of the pathway is ahead and slightly to the left. Walk up through fields and woods in a south-south-easterly direction, then follow the paved forest trail to the right. Go along the edge of some fields beside some woods for 800 metres and take a very winding path on the right. This leads to the D100 road. Turn left onto this to the village of Leguillac-de-Cercles.

Leaving the village by the eastern end, turn left taking the road to Les Tremblades, and go as far as the church. Take the paved track heading south-east as far as a sort of pass (180 metres high) where you will have a panoramic view over the wide tributary basin of Le Boulou at the foot of La Gonterie-Boulouneix hill.

Where the road bends at the summit, leave the paved track and turn right, onto a country path fringed with fields and embankments. A little way beyond Les Piles farm leave this path and go left to a small wood. Some 600 metres further on, this will bring you to a road. Go right and you will come to a hamlet called La Verrerie.

Detour *30 mins*
PAUSSAC-SAINT-VIVIEN
⌂ ⚑
Follow the road south.

4Km
1

Boulouneix
*Small village with a
Romanesque church
undergoing restoration.*

8Km
2

Go into the hamlet and at the square, turn left out of the village and follow a path flanked with low stone walls leading down to a wood, over a footbridge and on in the direction of Le Boulou. Keep along the edge of a meadow. Join a dirt path at the bottom of the valley and go left along it, passing by the cliff of La Verreterie-Tabaterie (prehistoric deposits, little cave in the overhang at the top of the cliff). Go up the valley to Tabaterie. The track zigzags around the base of huge rocks. Keep along side the rocks, then climb up the hillside through the box trees. The footpath bends right, then take a track, flanked with stone walls, which eventually becomes a forest path. Skirt another ridge for about a kilometre. You now come to a road. Turn onto this road heading right, as far as Boulouneix.

Beyond the church, go down past the cemetery to the road. Follow this road as far as the fork, turn right and go along to La Suchonie. Some 200 metres beyond this little hamlet, leave the road and go straight ahead into a wood, then follow a winding, paved track which climbs upwards. The path goes between fields and woods, coming out at the corner of a cultivated plot of land with a forest path at the edge. The right-hand direction leads to the Saint-Julien-de-Bourdeilles road.

The GR turns, and after about 200 metres, you turn right onto a country track which goes into a wood. The path turns eastwards, crosses a road near a place called Le Pic, and 500 metres further on comes to a crossing in the forest. Turn right and then immediately left (east) onto a stony road leading to a T-junction. Take a path to the right, leading into the woods. Some 350 metres further on, turn left and go down into the valley, taking the footbridge across the diversion. Walk back up the other side and turn left onto the path which skirts northwards along the ridge overlooking Brantôme. Join a footpath which hugs the hillside. This leads to Rue Pierre-de-Mareuil. At the next crossroads, turn right to the abbey and town of Brantôme, via the 'Porte des Réformés'.

BRANTÔME

CHAMPAGNAC-DE-BELAIR

LAFARGE

Château de Puyguilhem
The château is listed as a building of historical interest. It is closed on Tuesdays; follow the waymarked trail.

SAINT-JEAN-DE-CÔLE

Beynac

SAINT-SAUD-LACOUSSIÉRE

Detour GR436 Brantôme to La Mazaurie (on the GR4).

The GR436 leaves the D82 and cuts through to the hamlet of La Faye. From there a track leads through woods and fields to the ruined abbey at Boschaud. A narrow road goes from there to a nearby hamlet.

The GR footpath goes down to the Château de Puyguilhem.

Opposite the château, take the D3 road to the right as far as Villars. Leave Villars by the D82 road, but turn off to the left after a short distance and go up to Bionac and Lavergne. Take the D82 again for about 300 metres, in the area of the Villars rock-shelters (Grottes de Villars), and turn right onto a track which is tarmac at first and then becomes earth. This runs through forest for 4 kilometres to the D98 road, crosses over and continues along a metalled track to a hamlet which overlooks the Côle valley. The GR drops down to a village.

The GR leaves the village via the Saint-Martin-de-Fressengeas road, going under the railway and climbing left to Vieux-Bourg. On reaching the N707 road go along it to the right. After some 300 metres turn right to Lespinasse.

The GR then crosses the D98 road and continues as earth paths along a wooded ridge to a tiny place called Peyrelevade (spot height 304). It then crosses the Mazeroux road at Bonnefond and stays on earth paths to Beynac.

The footpath skirts south of Beynac and then runs through a number of large, enclosed fields before coming to a road which leads to the hamlets of Les Bordes and Les Farges. It swings north and then west, crossing the Dronne near an old mill. It then follows the bank of the Etang de la Garenne and comes to the village of Saint-Saud-Lacoussiére.

The route of the GR436 leaves Saint-Saud heading north on the D67 road as far as the Grand Etang de la Gourgousse. It then uses

39

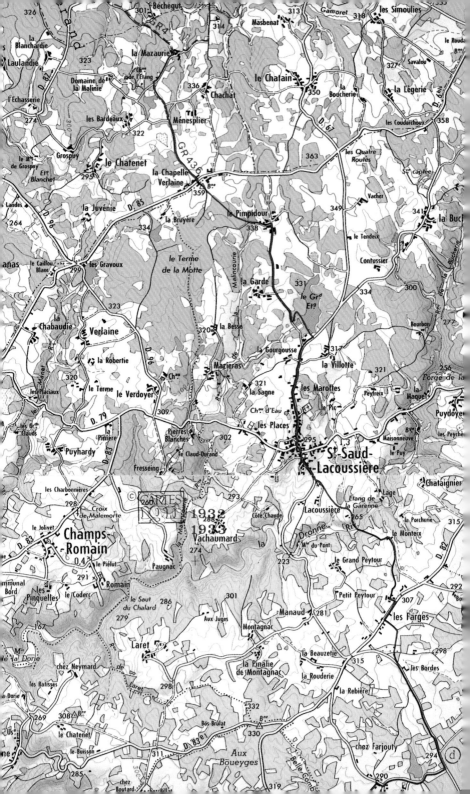

8Km
2

the embankment of the mere to reach a road, which it follows to Pimpidour. From there it takes a made-up pathway to La Chapelle-Verlaine, crosses the D85 road and heads along a road towards the hamlet of La Mazaurie.

La Mazaurie
Situated on the GR4 south-west of Pensol.

To continue on the GR36 you should return to Brantôme. Alternatively the GR4 heading west returns to Puymoyen.

The walnut

The production of walnuts for domestic consumption has long been an important source of income for smallholdings. Traditionally walnut trees are planted in scattered sites in or around fields. This hinders mechanized harvesting and makes it tempting to fell the trees especially as walnut is so highly prized for cabinet-making. Walnuts are gathered from September to the end of October by beating the tree with rods. A few walnuts are sold fresh, but they are mostly spread out in thin layers to dry. Large quantities of green walnuts used to be crushed in mills to make walnut oil. Although at one time walnut oil was an ingredient in regional cooking, it is not made or used very much nowadays. Almost as hard to find these days are walnut crackers, consisting of a hand-held mallet and a small wooden board held at an angle on the knees.

The truffle

The truffle, which boasts a long-established reputation, came into its own after 1880, as an economic substitute for the vine in the aftermath of the phylloxera; the disease which decimated vines. It is classified as a cryptogam (a plant having no stamens or pistils, and therefore no true flowers or seeds) and grows in limestone soil, mainly beneath oak trees, when atmospheric conditions are right.

The spores of the truffle germinate in the spring among the roots of oak trees. The truffle is produced from July-August onwards. They begin to shoot when the combination of warmth and moisture is right, reaching full size from about October between 5 and 40 cm below ground. The presence of the 'mushroom' is revealed at the surface by a patch of soil called *brûlé* or *brûlis* (scorch) on which no plants grow.

Harvesting, called locally *cavage* (digging), can begin at the end of autumn. Dogs and sows are good at locating ripe truffles, which are then simply dug out with a small pick.

Truffle production slumped dramatically after the turn of the century. But in 1970, French and Italian scientists discovered 'mycorrhiza', an organism controlling interchanges between the tree and the truffle. The French National Institute for Agronomy Research then developed a process for producing 'mycorrhized' oak saplings carrying this organism.

Since then, mycorrhized oaks and faster growing hazel trees have been planted. For this black mushroom, described by the Ancient Greeks as the '*Food of the Gods*', rescue is on the way.

BRANTOME

🏠 Ⓐ ✕ ♨ 🚋 🅱

5.5Km
1:30

VALEUIL

🍷 ♨

*Romanesque church. You
may wish to clamber to the
rocky point overlooking the
Fourneau du Diable and
enjoy a lovely view of the
valley.*

4Km
1:10

BOURDEILLES

🏠 Ⓐ ✕ 🍷 ♨ 🚋 🅱

*Picturesque township by the
Dronne; Middle Ages and
Renaissance château, one of*

Leave the town heading towards the cemetery, the GR436 goes up the left bank of the Dronne, climbs over Subreroche promontory, drops back down to the road and climbs again to Puyjoubert hamlet. From there it goes through woods to a little place called Valade, crosses the Côle and continues along the right bank as far as Petit Roc, then takes a made-up track through the woods to Condatsur-Trincou. It then uses dirt paths and comes to the D82 road at Saint-Marc, near a village.

On the left beyond the bridge are waymarkers for footpath GR436, which begins at the market place, Champ de Foire. It is possible to rejoin the GR4 at the hamlet of La Mazaurie between Abjat and Pensol (Haute-Vienne) via La Vallade, Boschaud abbey, Château de Puyguilhem, Villars and Saint-Saud.

Walk through the park beside the River Dronne and take the underpass to a path which runs parallel to the road. Follow this path through open country for about a kilometre to Vigonac mill. Cross a local road and walk to the left up a forest path which goes over the ridge and down the other side into a small valley fringed with prehistoric rock-shelters. The GR crosses the valley and climbs up again to the hamlet of Labrousse. It emerges onto a road. Go straight along it for 150 metres, then turn right onto a dirt path which links up with a local road in the valley. Go left on this local road. It leads via Amenot mill to a little town called Valeuil.

Leave Valeuil by the bridge over the Dronne and join the 'Route des Rochers' (Rock Path) heading west towards Bourdeilles for about 150 metres. Then turn right onto a forest path which returns to the road near the prehistoric site called Fourneau du Diable (Devil's Furnace). Follow the road for about 1,500 metres. Beyond Les Bernoux, take the path above Bourdeilles. This path leads down to the old bridge over the Dronne.

Leave the Bourdeilles via the market place and cemetery, heading south-east on the Biras road. After a short distance, turn left onto the path for Les Girards. This crosses a large cultivated plateau and heads towards Les

the four baronial seats of Périgord; 12th century church; old bridge and baronial mill.

10Km
2:30

BUSSAC
♟ ♨

6Km
1:50

Merlande Priory

Merlande priory was founded in the 12th century in the forest of Feytaud by monks from Chancelade abbey. It was destroyed by Protestants during the Wars of Religion and rebuilt, only to be sacked once again during the Revolution. The fortified chapel and the prior's house have been

Baconnets and Vaure where there is a reservoir. The path then goes through the woods towards a hamlet called La Chauterie where there are impressive views. About 200 metres before reaching the houses, bear right down a ridge and between the buildings of the derelict Guibaudie farm. Continue west along the valley bottom as far as the Biras road. At this point a bridle path waymarked red-orange shares the route of the GR footpath. Go left along the Biras road. Continue for about a kilometre, skirting the grounds of the Château de la Côte, and then turn right onto a path which leads across country to the little hamlet of La Courélie.

A country footpath heads southwards from there, down to the Bussac-Biras road. Take this road heading right for 200 metres. On the right is a footpath which goes through some woods and comes out again onto the same road. Turn right on reaching this road again and walk another 900 metres down to the little town of Bussac.

Turn left at the church, walk about 50 metres and turn right, taking a footpath up the other side of the valley and through the woods to Puyjean farm. Make for the D2 road below this farm. The footpath goes up again via Tamisier to the tiny hamlet of La Lande and comes to a road. Cross the road and go down a gated path, carefully closing the gate behind you! A footpath goes down through woods and heather into a valley, coming to a tarmac road. Take the woodland path opposite which leads to Merlande Priory.

Detour On the left is the starting point of a minor footpath (PR), which is especially popular with walkers from Périgord. (This can be followed from the map.)

5.5Km
1:30

restored. The chapel is a Romanesque building with a two-tier nave; the choir is surrounded by arches with decorated capitals.

Follow the road for 500 metres. Turn right and follow a paved footpath up through the woods to a clearing called Le Fuselier, skirting it for some 200 metres. At the end of the clearing, go down a woodland track onto a forest path on the valley bottom. The GR continues along the marshy floor of this little valley and then climbs up again to the D2 road.

On the right is the starting point for the Isle Valley footpath, GR646, leading south-west to Sainte-Foy-la-Grande.

Follow the D2 road left for 80 metres. At about this point the GR joins up with the PR detour from Merlande Priory. Take the footpath off to the right to Les Chicoins keeping the water-tower on the left. The footpath heads south-west through a wood and comes out at a building development.

Go right, onto a forest pathway up to a wooded ridge from which you can see, nestling in its little valley, the small town of Chancelade.

Detour
PÉRIGUEUX

Administrative capital for the Dordogne.

CHANCELADE

Abbey founded in the 12th century and reconstructed in the 15th and 17th centuries; museum of religious art; Romanesque chapel of Saint-Jean; prehistoric rock-shelter at Le Raymonden where 'Chancelade Man' (Magdalenian) was discovered.
Son-et Lumière at abbey; display of son-et-lumière at Chancelade. 12th century Augustinian abbey.

Detour From the abbey you can go straight to Le Gour-de-l'Arche, about 1.5 kilometres away, by following the narrow road which heads south onto the 710 road. Buses run from there to Périgueux. Walking distance from Le Gour-de-l'Arche to Périgueux railway station is 4 kilometres.

Périgueux

 Périgueux famed as the capital city of foie gras and the truffle. It is also a city where Roman remains include the tower of Vesuna, a temple to the guardian goddess; the Norman gate; 3rd-century arenas and traces of the original Roman walls. The Middle Ages gave it one of the most unusual cathedrals in France, Saint-Front, roofed with domes and built in the plan of a Greek cross. This gives it a Byzantine appearance. The 12th-century church of Saint-Etienne also has domes. On the western side is a 10th century church in Latin style and a cloister which has been converted to a gemstone museum. The banks of the Isle and the whole of the old town around the cathedral have retained many ancient houses and buildings. Prehistoric remains are housed in the Périgord Museum, and arms, armour, uniform, etc. are to be seen in the Musée des Gloires of Périgord.

Walk 100 metres along the road leading off to the right from the north side of Place de l'Abbaye de Chancelade and then go onto a grassy path, cross the railway, turn right and cross a stream called the Beauronne. The trail comes out onto the D939 road in the tiny village of Grèzes.

3Km
0:45

Head south on this road for 50 metres, then turn left between two small gardens. A fairly steep footpath leads, amongst other places, to a viewpoint overlooking the valley and the prehistoric deposits.

The footpath then enters woods. On the high ground it crosses Puy-Ferrat forest development and intersects a road. Continue straight ahead on a grassy track, then beneath trees, to top of the hillside. Turn left until you come to a field and a small derelict house, then turn right and skirt round the edge. Keep on this path to the hamlet of Beaupuy.

Turn left onto a road which gives a lovely view of Périgueux and the valley. Beyond Barbadeau is another Roman road. Turn onto this heading right. Walk another 100 metres and turn left towards Vignéras.

Vignéras

Detour 45 mins
Périgueux
Head right (south) along this road.

After a short distance take a short cut down to the D3 road and head left. In 150 metres turn right along a road leading to a splendid avenue of trees, into which the footpath turns left for a kilometre. On leaving the woods continue straight on alongside a meadow, then take a road going up to the right. On the right is the Château de Borie-Petit, headquarters of the Périgord Riding School.

3Km
0:45

Turn right, then left, and you come to Champcevinel.

CHAMPCEVINEL
🏠 ✕ ⛺

Cross this small town and walk along the road. It goes north-east at first, but then turns fully east and heads towards a radio booster station. After another 1.5 kilometres, turn towards Réjaillac for 100 metres, turn right towards La Grange and continue to the D8 (Route Napoléon). Cross the road and walk along an avenue of trees. On the left is the Château de Sept-Fons.

51

7Km
1:45

Les Gourdoux

Caussade
*Unusual 14th-century
fortified castle with
surrounding walls forming a
polygon.*

Go through a gate and continue beneath the trees for about 750 metres, You then come to a slope with a view over the Isle valley and the industrial parks at Trésillac and Boulazac. A pebbly footpath leads to a little place called Chaumardie. Go down to the quarry.

Turn left along a paved footpath heading north along the valley. After a kilometre, turn right and follow the footpath through the trees to a little farm. Go straight ahead and some 200 metres further, turn right, coming out in the small village of Les Gourdoux.

Turn left, then right and head towards the forest shadowing the horizon. On the left is the Château de Lauterie. At the first right-hand bend, keep going straight down along the edge of the woods. After 500 metres leave the track and turn right to follow a footpath through the woods leading to an avenue of trees. You are now entering the Lanmary State Forest.

If you stay on this avenue for a kilometre and then turn left you come to a very pretty spring. The water is not fit for drinking, but it is an ideal spot for a break or a picnic.

Go up the hillside along a steep path through the trees (waymarkers are not plentiful in this area), to a track overlooking the rooftops of the Château de Caussade. Turn left onto it, then right and you come to the château itself.

Walk along by the enclosed area and turn right to follow a pebbly, grassy track between forest plantations. In a kilometre, cross a narrow road and walk along the fine avenue of mature trees leading to the Château de Lanmary. This is a large lodge with towers on either side and wings jutting forward at right-angles. It is not open to visitors.

Skirt to the right of the château and its out-buildings, then take a footpath through the trees. After making a wide turn this footpath comes out onto a road. Turn left onto this road for 100 metres. Keep going in the same direction along a footpath which is mainly in open country for about 2 kilometres. Note the

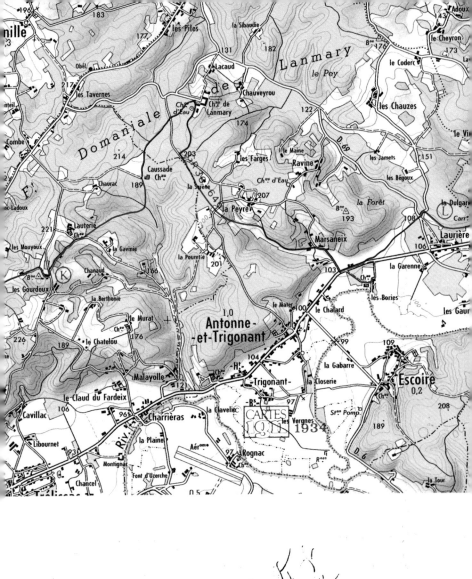

view to the right across Périgueux. Cross narrow road and come to the hamlet c Marsaneix 2 kilometres further on. Go dow into the valley to the N21 (Périgueux t Limoges road). Go left onto the N21. After few metres there is an avenue to a châtea dating from the 15th century.

7Km
1:40

Detour
Château des Bories

This château dates from the 15th and 16th centuries. It is open to visitors on request at the discretion of the owners, M and Mme de Lary, who have very kindly allowed a concessionary footpath through their grounds. The path leads right round the château and returns to the N21.

For the GR36 proper, go left onto the N21 a described above. Walk some 500 metres, the turn left onto a dirt path from which you ca look back at a fine view of the Château de Bories.

Follow this path to the intersection with the D69 road.

Detour
cemetery
dating from 500-751AD.

Detour see left. At the junction, cross the D69 towards Les Chauzes hamlet about 2.5 kilo metres away. Some 300 metres to the right c this little village is a necropolis of the Mero vingian period with many sarcophagi.

Keep going for 200 metres, then turn right ont a wooded pathway leading to a quarry, whic you overlook on your way to the N21 road where you come out in the tiny hamlet c Laurière.

LAURIÈRE
🏠 Å ✕ �×

A hamlet within the district of Antonne. Part of this walk goes alongside a quarry. Keep a careful eye on children at that point.

On the right, take the N21 towards Périgueu for 100 metres and then turn left down a littl street leading to the D69 road. Go left alon the D69 and cross the Isle. Some 750 metre further on, turn right (south) onto a pave track. This brings you to Combe de la Barg farm. Take the track to the main road and g right, coming to another road and turning rig again (west).

5Km
1:30

In another 250 metres, turn left along a pat which leads through woods to the little villag of Lauterie. There is a lovely view over th Auvézère valley. Go through Lauterie and wa parallel to the road for 100 metres, then take

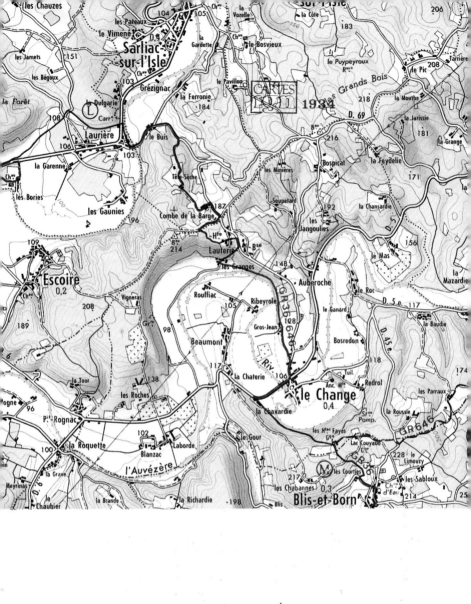

Referme les clôtures !

LE CHANGE

✕ �… 🍷 ⛲ 🚌

A small, picturesque village in the Auvézère valley. 12th century Romanesque church; Château dating back to the 15th and 16th centuries; some typical old Périgord houses.

2Km
0:40

Detour
Auberoche

Follow the D5 road left for a kilometre, coming to a chaep and the remains of the 12th-century fortress of Auberoche which was levelled by the townsmen of Périgueux during the Hundred Years War.

Junction
GR646

1Km
0:15

BLIS-ET-BORN
⌂

13th century presbytery.

4.5Km
1

potholed track to the right which goes down to the river. Beyond the quarry, turn left onto a rough, undulating track. The track first follows the river and then climbs again. It comes out into a clearing and then resumes its climb through trees to a meadow. Ahead is a forest path leading to Gros Jean farm. Go along to the left of the buildings and come to the village of Le Change.

Cross the Le Change bridge, then another bridge, and go along the D5 road as far as La Chavardie. Turn left and go straight ahead up through the wood overlooking the Auvézère. When you reach the top at Les Hautes Fayes, go along beside a meadow on the edge of a wood, then into the wood, coming eventually to a fork.

The GR36 takes the right fork and goes down through the pine trees. It then takes a track leading up through a meadow and brings you to a narrow road. The left-hand direction leads to the village of Blis-et-Born.

Leave Blis-et-Born heading south along a track which winds through the fields between walnut and apple trees. Go down a stony footpath through the gorse, then between pine trees, to a narrow tarmac road. Take the path on the other side of the road which climbs again, via La Gondie, through a pleasant little valley, passing to the right of Chignaguet hamlet on your left. After another 100 metres up the tarmac track, take a paved track off to the right, which leads through fields and orchards. At the top of this track, among some trees, we come to a narrow tarmac road leading to

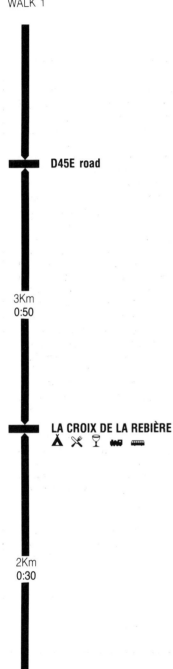

D45E road

3Km
0:50

LA CROIX DE LA REBIÈRE

2Km
0:30

eyliac. Cross over it, going straight ahead and then follow the path down among the pine trees to a spot where a number of footpaths intersect in a thick coppice. Go left along a track through a splendid example of underbrush and rejoin the eyliac road. Turn sharp right, skirt along the edge of the wooded area and then follow the footpath in among the trees to the road.

Cross this road and follow a woodland path to a large clearing. From here cross the clearing and go to the right, onto a path which widens and runs through a large wood for 600 metres. On leaving the woods you come to an intersection on the edge of a barbed-wire enclosure. Go forward along a paved track which leads to the tarmac road to Leygalie.

The first few houses at Leygalie are out on their own. Turn left just beyond them, then right, and take a track lined with enormous oaks. Follow the tarmac road for Milhac railway station and then take the path to Loubatières on the right, down into the woods. This will take you to the railway line. Walk under the railway through a white stone culvert. From there you must cross the Manoire stream by the bridge at La Croix de la Rebière.

Some 600 metres to the left is Milhac station on the Périgueux-Brive railway line; follow the N89 for a kilometre towards Brive for La Pélonie camping site.

Go left along the N89 for about 30 metres. Well before reaching the transformer turn right, onto a track which leads up through the edges of a wood. Cross a field onto a plateau, and on reaching the road turn right towards La Reynie. The road straightens out and comes to an intersection. Go straight over towards Mordèse on a track through meadows and thickets, coming eventually to a vine (on the right) and a group of tall trees. Turn left along a hedge which bears to the right alongside a field of geese and stay on this track as far as La Nane hamlet.

La saussa vielha

When conversation turns to good food in Périgord, you may hear talk of *la saussa vielha*(1). You see, once upon a time in Périgord people didn't eat meat whenever they felt like it, the way we do now. They only ate meat once a year, at Carnival (Shrove Tuesday), and what was left had to be buried next day, because it was the first day of Lent. But when they did eat, they ate!

First they had some nice fatty soup, then cleaned the plate with a little splash of wine from a jug (just enough to fill the middle of the soup plate), and because that went down well, and to do justice to the cook, everyone had some more, and cleaned their plates with just another touch of wine. Then they had a huge, helping of boiled meat *entre gras e magre* (neither fat nor lean) with a big chunk of bread, followed by a quarter chicken in the pot (not quite a royal feast, but close) and a good chunk of stuffing. Next they had a daube, that local meat stew without which no meal was properly 'saddled and bridled', as they used to say in Périgord. This daube had been cooked slowly in a deep pie-dish, with fire above and fire below, and the sauce was a glory to behold, because beef and carrots had to be good and fat, and it was so good *que lo babinho n'en gotava* (your chin could taste it). To round off the meal there was a lovely home-made pie, something they call where I come from *un pasti*, a huge fruit tart also cooked in a deep pie-dish with fire above and below, with a crust two fingers thick on top, and a crust two fingers thick underneath, crammed to bursting with cooked apple or prunes. And everything liberally washed down with our lovely wine from the Périgord hillsides. I know everyone says the wine is impeccable where they come from, but it wasn't always so round here. Sometimes it did taste just a little of the wood, and sometimes it was perhaps a touch on the sour side. In upper Périgord it was even a bit acid. But at any rate it was always the best in the district.

Then they would have a nice cup of coffee, and wash it down with a pousse-café, that's to say two fingers of eau-de-vie in the bottom of a glass. This would be washed down with a rincette, that's to say two fingers of eau-de-vie in the bottom of a glass. This would be washed down with a sur-rincette, that's to say two fingers of eau-de-vie in the bottom of a glass. Then just to round things off, they would wash that down with a gloria, that's to say two fingers of eau-de-vie in the bottom of a glass. . .

After which — they went for a little lie down. And no sooner in bed than it felt as though someone had sneaked into the room and jumped on their chest, with knees pressing down like lead, until they felt. . . smothered. All they had was a touch of *saussa vielha*.

MARCEL SECONDAT

From Contes et légendes du Périgord (Myths and legends of Périgord), published in Périgueux by Editions Pierre Fanlac.

1. The phrase cannot be translated literally. The meaning in English is akin to: over the top!

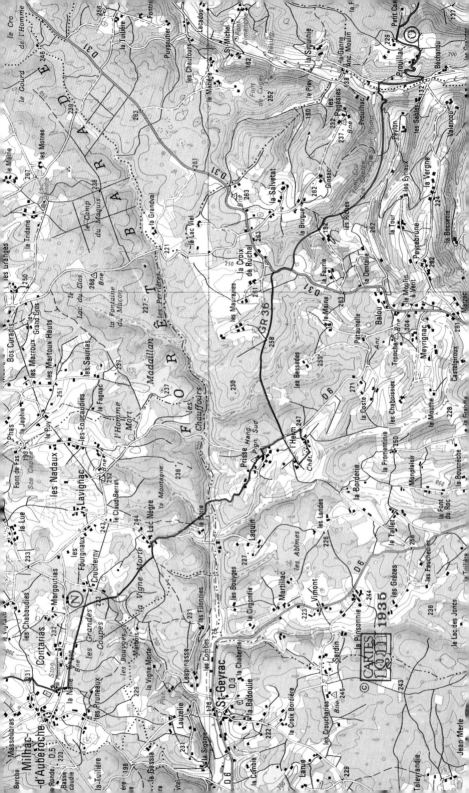

MILHAC-D'AUBEROCHE

3Km
0:50

Lac Nègre

Château de l'Herm
A very attractive ruined château dating from the Renaissance. It has lovely 16th-century chimneys and a magnificent spiral staircase. It is listed as a building of historical interest.

Keep straight along the tarmac road to the crossroads. Turn left and keep straight on for 400 metres. When you get to the bend, keep going straight ahead on a dirt path which was possibly a Roman road. Keep going for 800 metres across open country. Before you get to Cruciferny, on the edge of some woods, turn right and head among the trees. Keep straight on at the intersection. As you go down the track out of the wood, bear slightly left along by a hedge and then take a track which climbs up into the woods again. Keep going at the fork, bearing a little to the right. On leaving the woods, turn left onto a sunken pathway leading to the hamlet.

Turn right, down the road flanked with chestnut trees, as far as a white road. Turn left onto this road and follow it among the pine trees for 250 metres. Keep straight ahead on a grassy track, bearing to the left of La Borie hamlet, and go down through the untamed woodlands of the Forêt Barade.

Keep going along the bottom of the valley for a short distance, then walk up again to the right through a grassy clearing overgrown with pine trees, gorse, heather and furze. You will then come to a track leading onto the plateau among the outbuildings and houses of Prisse village.

To continue with the GR, face the Château and turn left off the road onto a pathway among trees. This crosses a dirt path and some fields, then once more enters the trees. It comes out onto the D31 road where you turn right for 100 metres. On the edge of a wood, skirt to the left around a field, go in among the trees and walk down into the valley along a footpath which is wet in places. At an intersection, keep going in the same direction, Les-Riches farm is on the right.

In another kilometre you come to a pumping station and a large enclosed area with gates which is private property. Walk along to the end of the enclosure and keep going in the same direction as far as a tiny hamlet where

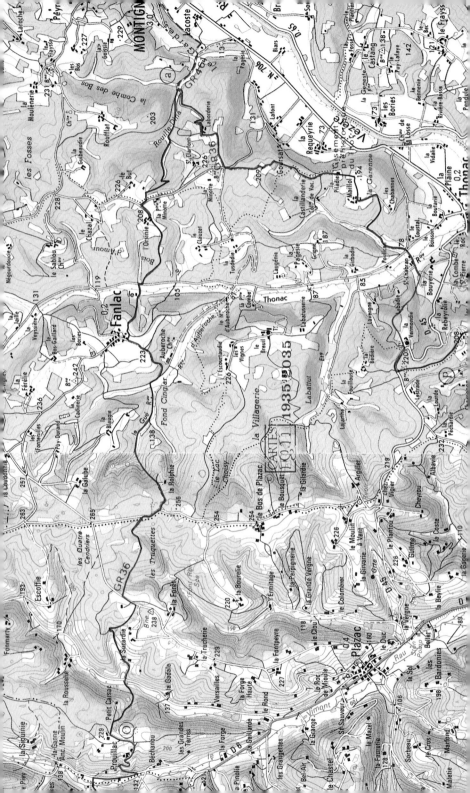

12Km
3:30

Fanlac

*Small village; 12th century
church with 17th-century
revisions; attractive
17th-century stone cross.*

4Km
1

you turn right, taking a paved track to the D6 road. Turn right and proceed to the Prouilhac crossroads.

A path leads left up to a farm. Walk past the farm buildings and stay on the hilltop path to a house.

Turn right into the woods and go down into a valley. Skirt a meadow, then take a wet, grassy path which comes out onto a road where you turn right. After 50 metres go left. A rocky footpath, shaded in summer, goes up in the direction of Le Cros and La Suzardie on the right.

At the top of the slope you come to a narrow road which you follow for some 200 metres. Care is required on this section, there is no means of waymarking the trail. There is no access to the right.

On the edge of the wood leave the road and turn right by a vineyard. The footpath goes into the trees for a kilometre, the trail is not very obvious, but is carefully waymarked. On leaving the wood the path winds between cultivated fields. It then becomes grassy, then rocky. At the next intersection, you turn left and come to a road. Turn right onto this road for 500 metres. Turn left under the trees again, along a track leading to La Rolphie, the farm is on the right. Keep going in the same direction along the edge of some meadows, then drop down into the valley along a winding, over-grown pathway.

Cross a stream and follow the path through open country overlooking some meadows. Where the paths cross, leave the valley and turn left up a pathway which overlooks the Château d'Auberoche. At the top of the hill, make your way towards Fanlac.

As you enter the town, turn right and follow a track down into the Thonac valley. Cross the river and a road, then go up through the woods towards L'Orsinie. Keep to the right along a road for some 80 metres, then pass to the right of La Petite Minote and follow a grass·

track dropping down into a valley. Keep going till you come to a wide track, and there you will find the junction with footpath GR461 which connects the prehistoric sites of Lascaux, Le Regourdou and Le Thot.

Junction with the GR461

Alternative route to Terrasson-la-Villedieu. The GR461 connects the prehistoric sites of Lascaux, Le Regourdou and Le Thot. It is waymarked to the Dordogne and Corrèze boundary.

2Km
0:30

GR36 turns at an acute angle (south-west) whilst GR461 heads towards the valley of the Vézère (south-east). Some 800 metres further on it changes direction and comes to Montignac.

MONTIGNAC
🏠 🛉 ✕ 🍷 ⚒ 🛈

*Important tourist centre:
Lascaux, Le Regourdou, Le Thot.
The famous cave of Lascaux
which contains spectacular
prehistoric paintings and
carvings is 2 kilometres
away from Montignac. The
cave is now closed, but
Lascaux II a faithful model is
open. There is also an
information centre which
gives details about the
caves. There is a prehistoric
art centre at Thot.*

At the town centre, cross the bridge over the Vézère and go to the left of the mairie. About 200 metres beyond the Syndicat d'Initiative (Tourist Information Office) near an old church, take a narrow street off to the right (Rue du Barry) which leads to the road for Lascaux and Le Regourdou. Stay on the road up to Lascaux. Some 500 metres beyond a hairpin bend turn to the right onto a track which winds among the prehistoric sites.

The track leaves the woods, goes past the front of Les Compousines children's home and bends right, entering a sparse wood. It soon comes to a clearing. Before reaching the edge of the wood again, turn left onto a dirt path which leads to the hamlet of Les Combes. Turn right after some houses on the left, and after another 50 metres turn right again. Go down through the woods and come out onto the drive leading to the Château de la Filolie. Turn right, pass a transformer, and go up towards the château.

10Km
2:30

Château de la Filolie
Fine example of the Sarlat style.

Go past the front of the château and follow a paved track which joins the N704 Montignac to Sarlat road. Go left along this road for 100 metres and turn right, onto a paved track which runs along the valley for a kilometre and then goes up through some woods. Cross the road and head along the drive to La Genèbre farm. Go to the left of the farm. The track drops

down through some woods and as you leave them you come to a village.

SAINT-AMAND-DE-COLY
✕ ♨

Famous Romanesque abbey with monumental porch (listed as a building of historical interest). Saint-Amand-de-Coly is a bustling little village in the summer, with concerts and exhibitions.

4Km
1:10

Walk past the front of the church, turn left and follow the road up the hillside to the hamlet of Mortefond. Beyond the farms go straight ahead along a woodland track which eventually becomes tarmac just before it comes out into Coly.

COLY
▲ ✕ ♨

Attractive little village on the edge of the River Coly.

Cross the village, go right, cross the Condat-Salignac road and follow the tarmac track across the Coly. Walk up through some woods for a kilometre. Turn to the right, onto a paved track alongside the Maison Seule truffle-bed. Leave this track and take a very old trail down to the right through the woods, pass a collapsed culvert and go up the hillside to the flat area at the top. Near a ruined house, turn left towards the hamlet called La Barétie. Follow the road straight ahead, ignoring the Lintignac road on the right, and go down towards Terrasson.

6Km
1:45

After 500 metres, take the narrow road on the right to Les Soudes. Go down the old walled track linking up with the Terrasson-Chavagnac road. Go left onto the steep, narrow old road leading to the walls of Terrasson old town, and enter through the fortified gate. Turn right, go through an alley past the church and you come to the Hotel de Ville (Town Hall) and the embankment alongside the river Vézère.

TERRASSON-LA-VILLEDIEU
⌂ ▲ ✕ ♨ 🚌 🚃 ⓘ

A charming little town bisected by the River Vézère bordering the Dordogne. Fine 13th century bridge, listed as a building of historical interest. Gothic church; old streets; terrace with panoramic view over the Vézère valley. The Dordogne

To rejoin the GR36, you should return to the junction, beyond Montignac.

and Corrèze boundary is nearby, Brive is 22km away on the N89 road.

Junction GR461

6Km
1:30

The GR36 goes westwards along the tarmac path. At Laborderie, go along a pebbly pathway through the middle of the farm. This brings you to a five-way intersection. Head south along a country track with extensive views to the south-east and east across the Vézère valley and you will come to the deserted farm at La Piladie. A narrow track leads off to the right as far as Maillol where a road goes down to the left into the valley. Pass by a restored house and turn to the right along a country track through a wood. Leave this trail after a short distance and go left down into a valley, coming out onto a tarmac path. Turn to the left and follow it to the Thonac road (spot height 78 metres).

Thonac Road
Detour *20 mins*
THONAC
🏠
Take the road to the left (south-east).

6Km
1:30

The GR36 crosses the road and the stream and takes you to the Saint-Chabran windmill where you go off to the right. Some 50 metres further on, go to the left up a cattle trail which leads through the woods, eventually skirting to the right of the leaning tower at La Vermondie which is listed as a building of historical interest. This brings you to the D45 road, where you should head right, staying on the road as far as a transformer. There, go left onto a forest track leading to Hauteclair where you will have one of the loveliest views in the region over the valley of the Vézère. The GR36 then goes down to a small town.

SAINT-LÉON-SUR-VÉZÈRE
🏠 ⚓
Romanesque church; 16th-century Château de Clérans; 14th-century Château de la Salle.

The GR does not go into the town. It crosses the Vézère and goes back along the left bank some 1.8 kilometres. The footpath which skirts along the foot of some overhanging rocks is well shaded in summer. It passes a spring and comes to the prehistoric rock shelters of Castel Merle.

Castel Merle
Prehistoric rock-shelters open April-October from 9.00 a.m. to 12.30 p.m. and 2.00 p.m. to 7 p.m. At other times enquire at the hotel.

6Km
1:30

Turn to the left onto a narrow tarmac road. After 300 metres turn off from the Sergeac direction and go up to the right along a grassy track leading to the Hotel de Castel Merle.

The GR36 goes down into a valley, crosses a meadow, curves right and left then comes to Chaillac farm. Set off to the right, then right again and go down to the left along a narrow woodland footpath. Coming to a paved track, go left along it to the bottom of the valley. It heads north-west, skirts the hillside and comes out at Peyzac-Le-Moustier.

You come to the valley of the Vézère by the D66 road and cross the river to get to Le Moustier.

LE MOUSTIER

Ⓗ ✗ ⚍

Museum and prehistoric sites, open all the year round except Tuesday from 9.00 a.m. to noon and from 2.00 p.m. to 6.00 p.m. (visit lasts 30 mins).

2Km
0:30

At the church head left along a road leading to Sous-le-Ruth. Just before entering the hamlet, go straight ahead and up the hillside.

Sous-le-Ruth

The 'Marmites de Géants' (Giants' Cooking Pots) are open to the public (visit lasts 30 mins) on application to M. Roye. Tel. 53 50 74 37.

Go left down a track into a valley and you will come to a hamlet.

LESPINASSE

◻ ▲ ⚍

Detour *20 mins*

La Madeleine

Prehistoric cave-dwellers' village.
Follow the arrows to the right for 1.6 km and you come to the prehistoric cave-dwellers' village of La

2Km
0:30

Madeleine. Open 1 April to 30 September from 9.00 a.m. to noon and from 2.00 p.m. to 7.00 p.m. (visit lasts 45 min to 1 hour). Tel. 53 53 44 35. Either go back the same way to the main GR footpath, or to Les Eyzies by a minor footpath (PR) waymarked in yellow. Ask the guide, M. Deuscher.

The GR36 heads along the road towards some cliffs.

Cross the Vézère. Go to the right and walk some 300 metres along the N706 road, then go left (east) onto a tarmac path. The footpath skirts a house and heads south before going down to the village of Tursac.

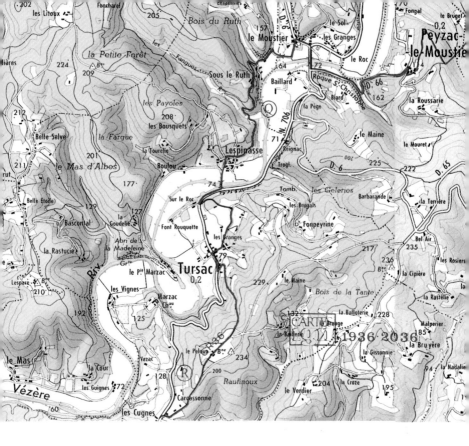

TURSAC
🏠 ⛺ 🍴 ⚓

6.5Km
2

Leave the village by the N706 road. Just outside the village take the pathway up to the left, which is tarmac at first, then paved. The footpath goes through some woods and climbs up to a height of 234 metres, near a pig farm. It then comes to Le Peloux, which is a good place to stop and admire the view across the valley.

The GR soon comes to a narrow road. Continue straight along it to Les Cugnes. Here the GR goes left along the N706 road for 100 metres and then goes up to the right along a track which is at first tarmac and then paved. Some 20 metres beyond a new house, go to the right along a forest trail which at first is not easy to spot. The path widens and skirts the hill. At La Grange go to the right and make your way down to Les Eyzies-de-Tayac where Walk 1 comes to an end.

LES EYZIES-DE-TAYAC
⌂ 𝗔 ✕ ⚓ 🚌 𝟮

*Musée National de la
Préhistoire, Musée de la
Spéléologie, natural
crystalline formations at
Grand Roc cave.
Prehistory tours depart from
outside the Tourist
Information Office (Syndicat
d'Initiative) at Les Eyzies
from June to September.*

The National Museum of Prehistory

The Museum stands on a long, rocky terrace above Les Eyzies. It was established here in 1918, among the ruins of the medieval Château de Tayac, on a site first occupied during the Late Magdalenian period. There are six exhibition halls (introduction with documents and charts, regional collections, tombs, artefacts in bone and stone, cave art), various reserve exhibits and a laboratory storeroom, making it one of the most interesting and informative museums in the world for both the layman and the specialist prehistorian. A statue of primitive Man (not, as is often mistakenly said, of Cro-Magnon man) stands on the edge of its terrace, from where there is a breathtaking view over the surrounding valleys, for so long the haunt of different prehistoric races. Into the distance stretches the cliff-face, its caves and rock-shelters now divested of their ancient secrets. It is well worth setting out on the walk signposted from the museum, for further on there is a magnificent view over the Beunes valley, and you can make your humble pilgrimage to the grotto of Les Eyzies. This cave (also called Richard's Grotto — Grotte Richard) was the source of some breccia fragments containing flints and reindeer bones, which were put on display by a mineralogist in Paris. These fragments were acquired by Edouard Lartet, the palaeontologist, and inspired him to go to Les Eyzies in 1862. There he carried out the first archaeological digs of the main deposits in this prehistoric capital. Later in this same cave, Denis Peyrony, an eminent prehistorian, discovered among other things a large accumulation of colouring materials, which suggested that he may have found a workshop used by prehistoric painters. *For information on opening dates and times: Tel. 53 06 97 03.*

WALK 2

LES EYZIES-DE-TAYAC

Musée National de la
Préhistoire (National
Museum of Prehistory),
Musée de la Spéléologie
(Museum of Speleology).
Natural crystalline formations
at Grand Roc cave.

At this point the GR36 crosses the *Alps-to-Ocean* footpath (GR6), which leads west to Sainte-Foy-la-Grande and east to Sarlat, Souillac and Figeac.

The GR36 and the GR64 to Domme, share the same route as far as Allas-les-Mines.

Take the GR6 to the Sarlat road and turn left onto it for 20 metres, then turn right and take a dirt track to two houses at the foot of the hill.

Go round to the right of the first house and take a grass footpath which goes up and to the right until you come to a spring and an electricity pole.

The path then goes upwards to the left, cutting its way through hemlock and cow-parsley, before opening out just as it enters the woods. Within sight of first house in the hamlet of Beune where there is an hotel, the path bends right. A little further on you come to a tarmac road, go left along it.

The GR footpath follows a narrow road along a ridge for 600 metres. At the fork keep going straight ahead, and at the end of a hairpin bend turn left onto a grassy track which climbs as it heads south.

Further up the slope, the path comes to a white path which shortly brings you to a tarmac road on a level with Pech Bertrou.

Detour *30 mins*
La Mouthe
If you follow the road it brings you to La Mouthe and its painted cave.

10Km
2:40

The footpath GR36 turns right on to the tarmac road and a little further on, turns left onto a paved track which heads straight south and goes down through woods to a narrow road, where you turn left for 700 metres. Where the road makes a sharp bend to the left, take a poorly waymarked track to the right. A little

further on it joins a forest road. Head to the right along this, go up through woods, and after about 500 metres turn left. When you come to a large field, turn right, on to a pathway which runs alongside this field. The route comes out on to a hilltop path. Go left along this to Petit Roc farm.

Keep going along the tarmac road. Some 80 metres further on, just beyond an electricity pole, turn right onto a narrow path which goes down into a little valley where there is a spring. The path then climbs again, towards a little place called Pechboutier. As you reach the outskirts, turn sharp right.

Leave Pechboutier by a paved track which goes between a wooden shed and a corn-drying store and heads south. After a short distance the route divides. Stay on the left-hand path. The GR veers east across country and after another 600 metres turns to the right, along the D48 road, heading for the D35. Turn right for 10 metres, then strike left off the road and follow a driveway leading to a house. At the first bend, leave this drive and keep walking straight on, following the old line of the track through the meadow. Rejoin the driveway and a little further on cross the D48 road. Keep walking along a tarmac road heading south. This brings you to the Blanchard farm, which is not shown on the 1/50 000 map. Keep heading south till you come to a fork on the edge of the plateau. Go down via the right-hand track with views over the Dordogne valley and walk into Saint Cyprien.

SAINT-CYPRIEN

Pleasant centre for country holidays, with picturesque little streets, a Romanesque church with 12th-century belfry-keep, and 14th-century additions.

5Km
1:15

From the church, go down to the main street and cross straight over to some steps which take you to a narrow street and on towards the railway station. Turn right at the station, head for the D48 road and keep along it to the River Dordogne. Before you reach the bridge, go down to the left and walk along the right bank of the Dordogne.

The GR36 and GR64 follow the old towpath to the bridge at Allas-les-Mines. In sight of the bridge, go left up to the road and cross the Dordogne, then turn left into Allas-les-Mines.

Allas-les-Mines

The starting point for GR64 to Domme (south-east) is not far outside the village.

9Km
2:30

Just before the church, take an alleyway up to the right. After a few score metres turn right, down towards a stream, and in a short while you will join a tarmac path. Follow this path upstream. Just before the last house, cut off left on to a pathway up the hillside. The pathway comes out on to a paved track. Turn right and follow it past the fork.

The starting point for GR64 to Domme, (south-east), is slightly up and to the left of this track. The GR36 stays on the paved track and climbs up to a crossroads. One of the roads which intersects here is the D50. Follow it heading across and to the right, to Berbiguières. Some 400 metres farther on, go left on to a tarmac road to Fournet. On reaching the outskirts of this hamlet, go down to the right along a sunken lane with hedges on both sides (former royal road). Keep going down for about 50 metres and you will come to a meadow. Skirt this and go left along a footpath for 100 metres, cross a fallow field at an angle before following the winding forest pathway among the trees. You then come to a wide track and turn left along this.

Go right, on to a path which runs alongside an area of fallow land and through some woods down a small valley. Just 10 metres this side of a little road, go left along a well marked trail which goes up through the woods and skirts a field before widening out. At the intersection turn right and, as you come out of the wood, you will come to the Louiller farm.

From there, head west down a road which further on follows a ridge for a kilometre. At a crossroads, turn left (south) and take a pathway down to a shack among the pines and junipers. Take a little path down to the bottom of the valley. Join a tarmac path and head left along it for some 200 metres, then turn round to the right and take a cart track crossing the valley to a group of trees. The path climbs up through meadows and then starts to wind, passing to the left of the château and houses at Marcousin, coming eventually to the Saint-Germain road. Walk through a chestnut-grove, heading right, and 250 metres before reaching

Marcousin go left, through some woods, up a clay path to a clearing at the top of the hill. From there go down to the right through the pines and across the fields, to Lolivarie village. Cross the D51 road and the valley, along a dirt track which goes under a culvert. Walk up again towards Pessarni hill following a trail with two sweeping bends. Some 100 metres beyond the farm turn right on to a tarmac path which passes to the right of a water tower. Take the second track on the left and head for La Truffière. This track eventually becomes private. At this point keep going to the right, down the hillside to the bottom of the Nauze valley. You then come to Lavergne, where a former mill has been turned into a fish farm.

Follow the road for a kilometre to the cross at La Robertie. Turn right, towards the old mill at La Robertie, and cross the bridge over the Nauze, coming to the village called Fongauffier.

FONGAUFFIER

A very ancient spring.

1.5Km
0:30

At the intersection between the roads, turn right on to a grass track which goes under the railway bridge and up the hillside. When the paths diverge, keep left. As the path climbs, you have a panoramic view over Sagelat and its little Romanesque church. At the end of the hill the path turns sharp right, up towards Tournehill; the map wrongly describes it as Tourneguil.

Follow this path, which twice becomes a terrace track flanked with dry stone walls, partly open and partly in shade, before reaching the D52 road.

BELVÈS

Fortified site said to have been the hilltop fort of the Bellovaci Gaulish tribe. Later it was an English stronghold built upon the remains of a fortified 11th-century castle (belfry, tower of the Auditeur, the castle gatehouse in Rue Rubigant, ramparts on all sides).

Typical 14th-century covered market in lime-washed chestnut. Pillory chain is still visible on one of the pillars. The church of Notre-Dame de Montcuq dates from 14th and 15th centuries.

9.5Km
2:15

The GR turns right on to the D52 road. At the top of the hill, take the second road on the left and walk round behind the stadium and the cemetery. On reaching the D54, turn right on to it. You are very close to the church of Notre-Dame de Capelou, a well known site of pilgrimage which has a 16th-century stone sculpture of the Descent from the Cross.

Some distance before the church, turn left on to a little tarmac track as far as some crossroads. Turn right towards the little hamlet of Grimaudou. Stay on the tarmac track down to the Saint-Pardoux church, which overlooks a wooded hollow. Follow the tarmac track for La Bessède forest and in about another 1,200 metres you will come to the remote Bournat farm. Now take a track up through the woods, then across heathland, over the plateau which has been reforested. Keep on at the first intersection (track H). On reaching track I (spot height 231) turn left on to it.

The path skirts a pond, then goes down into a little valley. At the bottom, cross over a little bridge made of wooden slats, close to where some pathways intersect. Turn right and follow a path which comes to a road. Follow this for 300 metres to another road. In sight of Labrunie hamlet turn right, walk to the right of it and proceed along a track flanked with walnut trees. Go down through a wood into the Couze valley.

Turn right and follow the D26 road for 100 metres. As you draw level with a café-restaurant, take a grass track on the left. When you come to a fork, turn right. The GR follows the line of the valley to the cemetery at Bouillac.

BOUILLAC
♟ ⚓

4.5Km
1:10

The path goes to the left up the south side of the valley. Go right at the first crossroads along a tarmac track to Gandil farm. Cross the farmyard and then take a road bearing left to the tiny village of Astor. Go straight ahead along a track carved in the earth by a bulldozer, and up into the woods. Head west, cross a rustic stone bridge over a stream and proceed to Saint-Avit-Rivière. Cross the D2 road and continue on a tarmac track to Borie. Some 150 metres further on, leave this track and take a cart track which goes straight on. After passing an old mill you come to Montferrand-du-Périgord.

MONTFERRAND-DU-PÉRIGORD
🏠 🏠 ✕ ♟ ⚓
Château dating from the 12th and 15th centuries; 16th-century house.

Go left along the road up through the village. Pass the market place and church. As you draw level with the château and 16th-century house, go to your left along a pathway. This is overhung with bushes in places, then skirts some crops and drops down beneath overhanging trees.

5Km
1:15

The GR footpath follows the edge of the wood, turns right and climbs gently. On reaching a pond, go round it to the left and eventually turn right onto a road. After another 100 metres turn left on to the road from Montferrand. Stay on it for 350 metres and then go right, through some woods, along a forest drive much used by roe deer. This brings you to a cart track running alongside ploughed fields and then comes to a little place called Laurencie. A narrow tarmac road goes down into the valley and meets the D26e road. Follow this to the right for 600 metres. Turn left onto the tarmac track up to Jean-de-Bannes.

Jean-de-Bannes
Here, the GR6E comes in from the right, linking the GR6 to the GR36.

3.5Km
1

Continue up the hillside, skirt round a small lake and take the cattle trails into a wood (closing the gates behind you). You come out into a meadow. Take the middle path into the wood, alongside another meadow, through a wooded grove, across yet another meadow from corner to corner, and once at the top you come to a little road.

SAINT-GRINGAUD
Å

5Km
1:15

Detour *45 mins*
MONPAZIER
ⓗ Å ✕ ♈ ⚓ ▭ 🅑
*English fortified town dating
from the 13th and 14th
centuries.*

7Km
1:45

The GR footpath goes to the left (north-east) along a road for 300 metres and turns right on to another road. At Couge the GR leaves the road heading south, turns east, then goes north-east and eventually south again through a little place called Le Roucou. Farther on, cross a little stream and on reaching the ridge you come to Peyrégude hamlet.

Beyond the village take a grass track off to the left dropping down to the valley. The path comes out to a tarmac road. Turn left and follow this for 200 metres, then turn right on to a cart track through woods, meadows and crops. This side of the D660 road you come to the detour for Monpazier.

Detour (see left). This is a waymarked road. Leave the GR36 cart track and take a dirt track to the left. Cross the D26E and take the tarmac road, turn right and head straight along this road, to Montpazier.

Leave the main square heading for the north-west corner, go down into the little valley and turn left on to a track which joins a road on the hill. Follow this road for 1,500 metres and rejoin the GR36.

Some 200 metres further on, cross the D660 road and go to the right of a garage, on to a dirt track which goes through some woods to a little road. Turn left on to this road for 200 metres. Turn left again and in another 50 metres take a cart track off to the right which goes through a wood and changes to a narrow, partially overgrown footpath. At the edge of the wood you come across a tarmac track for the detour from Monpazier.

Turn right and go down the Gaugeac road. In another 200 metres a road takes you to Maran. Go through this little hamlet and, on reaching the last house, turn due south down a forest drive into the Dropt valley which brings you to the D2 road. Turn right. Beyond the bridge at Roussie mill, the footpath turns left heading southwards up into some woods. At the top of the hill turn left. The path, which is not very well waymarked, skirts a clearing as far as the

BIRON

🍴 ♨

Famous castle. The Château de Biron commands extensive views over the surrounding countryside. This collection of buildings was constructed in various styles by the 14 generations of Gontaut Biron who have owned the château. Among former members of the Biron family was Charles de Gontaut, Duke of Biron. Although a favourite of Henri IV because of his outstanding service, he nevertheless plotted against his king. The first time he was pardoned, but the second time, when he refused to renounce on oath the conspiracy with Spain and Savoy, he was condemned to death and beheaded in the Courtyard of the Bastille in 1602. The château is famous for its Renaissance chapel; estates chamber with an immense kitchen, and the so-called 'receipt' building (Bâtiment de la Recette) to which the peasants came to pay their dues.

5Km
1:20

LACAPELLE-BIRON

🏠 ⌂ ⛺ 🍴 🍷 ♨ 🛈

Extensive network of GR footpaths in the surrounding countryside.
Intersection of the GR36 and GR636 footpaths. The latter links with the GR6 at Monbazillac

south corner, where it winds away into the woods, heads eastwards, continues straight along the ridge and then goes right (south) along a paved road to the hamlet of Biron.

Go down the street where the castle is and cross the road. Turn left from a little square on to a paved track and join the D53 road. Turn to the right and go along this road for 750 metres, then turn right and go into the wood along a grass track leading to Ballande. You are now entering Lot-et-Garonne. In another 500 metres, as you draw level with a large house, turn left towards a derelict hut. The footpath is poorly waymarked for a stretch. It goes along by a wood, crosses a plank bridge over a stream and climbs gently towards La Vayssière, using part of the access drive for a short distance. Then it goes up to the left again (north at first, then east) among the trees. It then takes the D150 road going right, as far as a place called Peyrenou. From there, leave the road and follow a track to Lacapelle-Biron.

The GR36 crosses the town and goes down to the valley of the River Lède, crossing it near the rugby ground. From there a track goes up and through a little hamlet. When the track comes out on to a road, go straight ahead along a surfaced drive which heads north towards Macate farm. Just before the farm, turn right, and follow an attractive trail through trees, meadows and vines to Lafage. From

10Km
2:30

SAINT-FRONT-SUR-LÉMANCE
🏛 🚌 🅿

The 11th-century Romanesque church was remodelled into a stronghold, probably by the Templars. Further 16th-century revisions during the Wars of Religion emphasized its war-like character. Remains of a priory.

9Km
2:45

there, follow a road through plum orchards and pine woods (to spot height 248), where you cross the La Sauvetat road. The next stretch of footpath is often muddy to begin with. After 2 kilometres of pine woods and chestnut groves you come to Naugarède where you take a road to the right. After 200 metres turn left on to a track which goes down through some woods for a kilometre. On reaching a road turn right and then left on to the D246 road. Follow the D246 for 300 metres, then go sharp right and left.

The GR footpath then follows a little track along the right bank of the Briolance. This comes out on the N710 road which leads left to Saint-Front-sur-Lémance.

The GR footpath skirts the north flank of the church and gives excellent views of the apse. It crosses the River Lémance, runs close to the station and goes over a level crossing, then skirts to the left of a quarry and a lime kiln. Some 400 metres further on, a track going up to the right leads to Badet. Here cross a paved track and bear right towards the picturesque hamlet of Bourdiel. Beyond the hamlet turn right and join the Péméjà road.

At Péméjà turn left and left again to the hamlet of La Poulétie. Beyond La Poulétie the very pleasant footpath continues heading generally south-east. Some 900 metres further on, swing left and climb gently, first following the edge of a field and then a very wet sunken lane, till you reach a little place known as Pech-Peyrou. In this hamlet cross the first road you come to and go between two farms. Keep straight on to another road and follow it to the left. It becomes a country by-road.

In the corner of a vineyard the GR comes to another road which you cross to take a forest drive through pine woods. This passes Lion d'Or farm and comes to a road. Follow this down to the valley floor until you come to the D158 road, where you turn left and cross the lower part of the village called Bonaguil.

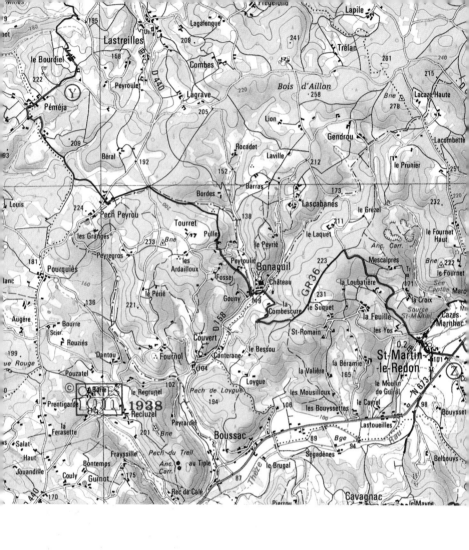

BONAGUIL

🍴 🍷

The 13th-century Château
de Bonaguil in
Lot-et-Garonne, on the Lot
boundary, is of special
architectural interest. Today
only the barbican and
courtyard can be seen. At
the end of the 14th century,
Jean de Roquefeuil rebuilt
the keep in the form of a
ship's prow turned towards

4Km
1

the north. To the west of the keep he built the baronial armouries. Early in the 15th century his son, Béranger, wanted to strengthen the castle's defences. He constructed all the other buildings along the lines of the traditional medieval fortress, even though at that time the first rays of the Renaissance were beginning to dawn. It is now a proud Gothic ruin, standing on a crag between two small valleys. It was destroyed during the Revolution by the ministrations of the Convention and the Biens Nationaux. Guided tours take place every day between Easter and 30 September, from 9 a.m. to noon and from 2 p.m. to 7 p.m. Shows of 'Son et Lumière' are put on between 1 July and 15 September. There are musical evenings from mid-July to mid-August. Artists' studio.

SAINT-MARTIN-LE-REDON

Country village along River Thèze. The church still has some of its original Romanesque architecture. Saint-Martial Spring.
At this point the GR36 crosses the GR652, which comes from Gourdon in the north and goes to La Romieu, the northern part of the pilgrim route to Saint James of Compostella.

4Km
1

The GR36 crosses Bonaguil stream. It goes to the right of the wash house and takes a wide paved track up through the woods. In another 200 metres it turns right and comes out on to a road. Go left along this road to the top of the hill, then turn left off it along a cart track. In another kilometre take a road to the right (south-west). Near a place called Les Yos, go left along the rural by-road for a few metres and turn right on to the path which goes down to Saint-Martin-le-Redon.

At a wayside cross take the V08 to the D673 road and turn left on to it. In 250 metres turn right up a road which eventually becomes a track through some trees. Take the next track on the left. As it leaves the wood it swings left (north) then right (east) on to a track beside some meadows. When you come to a road turn left. A little further on, go straight across another road to a sunken track. You then come to a road on which you keep going straight ahead. At the crossroads go down a cart track which runs parallel with the road, there is a lovely view across the plain and valley of the Lot. Go on to the bridge and left along the road, dropping down towards the mayor's office at Duravel.

DURAVEL
🏠 ⌂ ✕ 🍷 ▭ 🛈

*This little town is all that
remains of the extensive
baronial estates of Duravel
and of its church, around
which the abbey of Moissac
founded its leading priory in
the middle of the 11th
century. Opinions differ
regarding the number,
names and origins of the
'Holy Remains' currently
lying in the crypt beneath the
Carolingian sanctuary at
Duravel. What is known for
certain is that as the worship
of holy relics became
widespread in the Middle
Ages, so many visitors were
attracted that it became
necessary to construct a
substantial church over the
crypt and surround it with a
range of monastery
buildings. This crypt is one
of the rarest in France. It has
the appearance of a real
tomb, and, in its silent
darkness, crowds of visitors
came to worship. Some of its
capitals, now very worn, and
some early bases, come
from the original oratory
founded here about the
middle of the 4th century.
The stone flags, worn down
by the sandals and knees of
worshippers pausing to pray,
testify to the strength of faith
in those days.*

4Km
1

De Cazes chapel
⌂

From the mairie, head for the D911 road towards Puy l'Evêque. In about 250 metres go left, climbing gently up the 'royal road'. In another 400 metres turn left on to a track up the hillside. When you come to a cart track, go left along it for about 20 metres, then turn right and come to the old Le Tour farm. Turn right on to a road and in another 200 metres turn left, cross La Paillote stream and come to the group of houses at Cazabous. Go down a steep little lane on to the D68. The GR footpath crosses a bridge over the Cazes stream and goes past a chapel.

At the next crossroads turn off to the road going left. In 150 metres turn right and head up a tarmac road towards an iron wayside cross. Keep straight on (south-east). When you come to the D911 road, go right. In 100 metres turn left and go along the footpath beside the River Lot. When you come to the D911 again,

2.5Km
0:30

follow it eastwards. Having passed the roads department depot and a yard, go left up a road leading towards the top of Puy l'Evêque. Turn into the first street on the right. Go past the gendarmerie and the tax office, then follow another street with steps at the end, coming eventually to the D911 and the centre of Puy l'Evêque.

Puy l'Evêque

Puy l'Evêque was once called Podium, a Latin name for a hill with a more or less rounded top. This became Pech in Occitan, the local dialect, translated into French as Puy, to which the epithet 'l'Evêque' was added when Guillaume de Cardillac, bishop of Cahors, made the town an episcopal seat early in the 13th century. This is one of the most picturesque settings anywhere in the Lot valley above Cahors. Rows of old stone houses rise up like an amphitheatre from the right bank of the river. You get the best view of the town from the left bank of the Lot, near the suspension bridge entrance. Keeps, castles, fortified houses, churches, terraced gardens, elegant dwellings and steep streets combine to form an impressive collection of buildings.

Note in particular: the 14th-century church with 15th-century revisions and a porch-belfry entrance; in the cemetery, there is a wayside cross with ancient carvings.

Water transport in Quercy

The Lot — which is really an incorrect spelling of *l'Olt*, as is confirmed by local dialect, documents and place-names such as Saint-Vincent-Rive-d'Olt — was the first river in Quercy to be engineered for water transport.

The Gallo-Romans had everything wonderfully organized. They had rafts, ferries, boats and barges. These were manned and steered by oarsmen, boatmen and mariners of all kinds, who provided transportation by water. Among the various cargoes taken by barge down the Olt to Bordeaux were wines from the vineyards between Carjac and Fumel.

Following the Barbarian invasions, several centuries passed before the Lot was again used for navigation. The installation of locks and towpaths in the Middle Ages brought significant progress. With the construction of a fully integrated system of dams and locks in the 19th century, the canalization of the Olt was complete.

Once the Olt was fully equipped and engineered, it needed only to be inspected and maintained. Lock-keepers' houses were erected alongside every lock. Traffic started at dawn and went on until dusk, when the crews took to the taverns, inns and hostelries.

Water transport provided a livelihood not only for crewmen and hoteliers, but also for the carpenters, metal-workers and rope-makers who constructed the *sapines* (literally, 'deal tubs') and *gabares* (scows), as the vessels were known, as well as the drivers of animals, the longshoremen who carried goods on their backs, and the hauliers who delivered them to their destinations. The freight was mainly coal, iron, cast-iron and zinc from the Aveyron mining district, wood of various kinds from the 'high country', and wines from the Côtes du Lot. Vessels returned from Bordeaux laden with manufactured goods from the Gironde and around the world.

The most common type of barge was the *gabare*, heavily built of oak and practically indestructible. It had no keel, a flat bottom, and its sides were almost straight. In the stern, which ended in a dead straight, vertical bulkhead, was a deck house with a high roof. The cargo was stowed safely beneath protective decking. The capitani would stand in his deck-house with his hand on the tiller, giving orders.

Then suddenly, in 1887, maintenance and transport came to an end, just one year after the opening of the railway line from Cahors to Capdenac.

PUY L'EVÊQUE

4.5Km
1

Starting out from the Place de la Mairie, go past the terrace of a café-restaurant and down a winding path to the Rue des Capucins. Follow this street for 40 metres and turn right, taking first the Ruelle du Théron and then the Ruelle des Mariniers. These bring you to the Place de la Cale (formerly a port). From here, either the Rue de la Cale or the Rue des Rimottes will take you to the Place de la Liberté (mill). Take the Rue du Corps-Franc-Pommiès, cross the Grande-Rue and continue along the Rue des Platanes. At the crossroads

Rural houses in Quercy

Quercy has the most easily recognized style of architecture in France. The old dwellings on the plateaux of the Causse reflect the rustic way of life of the region. Houses in Quercy are ingeniously designed to cater for all aspects of family life, even including features to help their occupants to work the land.

A slightly sunken, vaulted ground floor called a *cave* (cellar) could be used as a wine store or sheep fold. The family accommodation on the next floor was reached by an outside staircase which was always made of stone flags. As often as not, it led to a terrace with an overhanging roof supported by wooden or stone pillars. This section was called the bolet. The original houses used only the natural materials of stone and wood. Effectively, they were even roofed in stone. Large slabs called lauzes were used, and these needed a specially shaped and strengthened frame. Today, flat tiles are used instead of slabs.

The most characteristic feature of Quercy houses must be the turreted pigeon house. Regarded as external signs of wealth, they have existed since the 13th century, when only the nobility were entitled to gather the much valued fertilizer, pigeon droppings, called locally colombine.

Between 1750 and 1850 pigeon houses became increasingly common, although the most unassuming devoted only the corner of their attic to pigeons, with just a hole for them to fly from, better described as a 'pigeon loft' or 'pigeon-gable'. Pigeon houses were sometimes built separately, but as often as not they formed part of the house. They survive today only as an architectural embellishment.

Another original feature of Causse houses is the little dry-stone wall marking the boundary of the home. Such walls can be seen following an unbroken line even through woods. Stones often had to be cleared from the Causse, and were used in the construction of little circular or oval buildings with conical, stone-flagged roofs. Such a shelter was called in the local dialect borie, cazelle, gariote or capitelle.

Whether making a refuge for people or livestock, an equipment store or an agricultural building, people learned over the centuries to build according to their needs and stations, using the materials to hand.

Stone shelter, Périgord

follow the D911 for about 100 metres. Turn left between the road and the sports ground changing rooms, taking the track for Belfas. Walk past 'La Clairière' and cross the 'Coustals de Pescadoire'. On reaching the road, go down it (admiring the fine views of the valley). At a crossroads keep straight ahead along the track across the the Font Cuberte stream. At the next crossroads turn left and then right, taking the Rue des Gabarets into Prayssac.

PRAYSSAC

This charming little town, which has become a centre for holidays and excursions, is also one of the most important business centres in the Lot valley because of its food-packing industry, especially foie gras and truffles, and the trade in Cahors wine.

4Km
1

Leave the village by the Boulevard du Maréchal Bessières. When you are level with the old market place, bear left along the Rue du Rouget. The GR footpath climbs up through trees to a very steep road. Go to the right along this for 500 metres and take a grassy track on the right, down towards the water tower and the village of Castelfranc.

CASTELFRANC

Stands at confluence of Lot and Vert.

Take the D911 road towards Cahors. Cross the River Vert (notice the trout farm on the right). Turn to the right up a paved track on to the plateau. In 2 kilometres you come to a road (near an oratory) and turn on to it heading right. Ignore the track leading left towards the hamlet of Fages. In a short distance, at a wayside cross with an iron crucifix, go to the left on a track which goes down at first and then goes up towards another wayside cross. Go down to the left. In 100 metres there is a bend, but go straight on along a path which joins a road. Cross this road and go straight

Castelfranc

The village of Castelfranc (free castle) reveals its past role as a Gothic stronghold in the geometric precision of its chequer-board layout. Fifteenth-century church with wall-belfry. On the walk you come to L'Impernal where archaeological research and digs on the plateau have shown that man had settled in this area by the 3rd century BC; that a Gaulish *oppidum* (hill town) with an enclosure 800 metres long and averaging 200 metres in width was installed here, naturally fortified by the fact that the ridge is in the form of an escarpment; and that the Romans built a double-walled enclosure on the spot.

ahead along a tarmac road which passes under an electricity supply cable. Some 300 metres further on the left you pass a megalithic tomb, turn to the right and take a grass track between stone walls, crossing a plateau with juniper bushes and a few oaks. When you come to a road, turn left on to it. In 20 metres take the first track to the right, then keep bearing right along a sunken lane. Cross a road. Keep straight ahead along a track leading to a place called L'Impernal.

Head left (south) along the shoulder of the plateau. The GR footpath follows the Lot, seen meandering over the plain below, and follows the edge of the *Cévenne*. It goes down to the bottom of a little valley, climbs and then drops down again towards the keep at Luzech.

LUZECH

Visit the old town districts of the Grand'Rue and the Faubourg du Barry; the five-tiered nave in the Church of Saint-Pierre (Saint Peter); Chapel of Notre-Dame de l'Isle (pilgrimage from 8 to 15 September); the La Pistoule way of the cross, much used at Ascension; the archaeological museum.

Cross the Lot by the Pont de la Douve (western bridge) and in 100 metres head left along the D88 Sauzet road. At the crossroads 250 metres further on, go left on to a tarmac track between farm buildings. In a short distance continue along the middle grass track alongside the Lot. Cross a stream (as often as not dry) and a little further on cross the Combe de l'Isle stream by a bridge made of logs. On the other bank you can glimpse the Chapel of Notre-Dame de l'Isle through the poplars. Continue along a paved track between the Lot and the *Cévenne* (spur with a very steep ridge). Beyond a mill, you come to the small village of Saint-Vincent-Rive-D'Olt.

8Km
2:0

3.5Km
1

Stone shelters

Various dialect words (borie, cazelle, gariote, capitelle) are used to describe these small, mainly round, dry-stone shelters with conical, stone-flagged roofs. They once housed equipment, crops, livestock and sometimes even people.

SAINT-VINCENT-RIVE-D'OLT

Church with a carved, 17th-century, wooden baptistry door; Maison Tardieu with two splendid windows; in the square, a 300-year old elm.

Leaving the church behind you, go up a narrow little street on your left which leads to the top of the village. Beyond the last house, turn to the right on to a paved track which goes along the hillside and eventually becomes a grass path. As you come to some new houses, turn left as far as the D23 road. Turn right on to this road. Ignore the D8 which

8.5Km
2

goes off to the left and, in another 100 metres, turn right on to a path which goes between some new houses. This path is flanked by oaks and fir-trees as it climbs up to a plateau. Keep heading in the same direction between stone walls and box-trees. Pass an electricity pylon and in 1,200 metres come to a road, and go left along it.

At a wayside cross turn left down a grass path to a road and the outskirts of a little place called Labouysse. Follow the road to the left. In 250 metres take a path with crops on the right and heathland on the left. Follow this path along the edge of the plateau. Cross heath

and woodland, arriving at the derelict hamlet of Mader. Take the road leading down to the right as far as the first hairpin bend. You will have views over the valley of the Lot with the houses of Douelle in the fore ground and the Château de Mercuès in the distance. At that point, go straight ahead along a path which bypasses the twists and turns in the road and comes out in a narrow little street. Turn right along it and enter Douelle.

DOUELLE

⌂ ✗ 🚉 🚌

This village was once the home of the boatmen who transported wines to Bordeaux; its economy now depends on agriculture (wine, strawberries, tobacco, walnuts, market gardening) and tourism.

From the church head to the right, then turn left. Between a bakery and a butcher's shop, turn to the right along a pathway (steps at first) which climbs towards a TV transmitter. Beyond the transmitter, turn left along the track to Les Cazes hamlet. Ignore a path on the left. Go down and up again to La Gourdonne farm. Keep straight on along a path flanked by box-trees, passing below an electricity supply line. In a short distance, bear left onto the path leading away from the supply line and go up the hillside to the plateau. At an intersection go straight ahead along a grass track.

8.5Km
2

In 500 metres you come to a road. Keep straight on and eventually the footpath becomes a paved track. Stay on the narrow road. There are two bends and the road then goes under the Roquebillère viaduct. Then turn right on to the pathway down the hillside. Pass the Hermitage Sainte-Quiterie, 17th-century former convent. The GR footpath reaches the road alongside the River Lot. Turn right and follow the road to the Valentré bridge.

A little further on, to the right, you will see waymarking for the GR65, the *Saint-James of Compostella* route, leading to Moissac, La Romieu and Eauze.

The GR36 does not go into Cahors. It continues along the tarmac towpath heading in the upstream direction.The GR36 to Villefranche-de-Rouergue and GR65 to Figeac share the same route as far as the plateau to the east of Cahors.Take the Valentré bridge if you wish to go into Cahors.

CAHORS

🏛 ⌂ ✕ 🍷 ⛏ 🚌 🚃 🛈

Of special interest: the Pont Valentré, the cathedral of Saint-Etienne, Quartier des Badernes, Quartier des Soubirous, the ramparts and a tour of the bridges.

Cahors

Cahors is the administrative capital of the département and region of Lot, and the capital city of the ancient territory of Quercy. The town stands in a bend of the River Lot at an average height of 130 metres. It was founded by the Gauls, and in Gallo-Roman times it became known, after the Celtic people who gathered at its spring, as *Divona Cadurcorum*, the sacred spring of the Cadurces. It was this tribe which held out longest against Julius Caesar during his conquest of Gaul. In the Middle Ages, Cahors became the leading financial centre in the Christian world. Its University was founded by Pope John XXII in 1332, making Cahors an important cultural centre, and during the same period the consuls ordered the construction of the remarkable Pont Valentré, still one of the finest fortified bridges in Europe.

Many relics have survived to confirm that this city regularly acted as host to pilgrims heading for Santiago de Compostela. First, there is the many-domed Romanesque Cathedral of Saint-Etienne (St Stephen) which was consecrated on 10 September 1119 by Pope Calixtus II and was built on the site of an earlier sanctuary. There were also several hospitals, one of which was called the Hôpital Saint-Jacques. It was close to the present-day Place Galdemar. Then in 1683 it was transferred to the place known as the Croix des Capucins. In the 16th century a chapel dedicated to the apostle of Spain became known as Saint-Jacques des Pénitents when it became the seat of a brotherhood of blue penitents. The town suffered many occupations and wars, but throughout the Middle Ages it was both a university town and a centre for merchants and money-changers.

Excellent regional produce has made Cahors a gastronomic centre, well-known for its truffles called locally *black diamond, cabécous*, potted meats and foie gras from geese and ducks, its mushrooms and its game dishes. Cahors wines come from *auxerrois*, one of the oldest vineyards in Gaul.

Cahors, Pont Valentré

WALK 3

CAHORS

(see map ref A)

5Km
1:30

Crossroads at Saint-Cirice

6Km
1:30

At the Valentré bridge the GR36 meets the GR65 without going into the city. The GR65 goes south-westwards towards Montlauzan and south-eastwards, GR36, as far as the Place de la Résistance.

On the left bank at Valentré bridge, the GR36 and GR65 go along the tarmac towpath heading upstream. You come to the Fontaine des Chartreux (reappearance of an underground stream fed by water-bearing strata beneath the Causse of Limogne) and walk under the railway bridge. This brings you to the N20. Go across this road and a small square.

At this point you part with the GR65, which heads south-east towards Figeac. At the foot of a statue of the Virgin Mary, footpath GR36 turns right and goes up a flight of steps which becomes a pebbly footpath to the Mont Saint-Cyr transmitter. From there take the road to the crossroads on the Saint-Cirice road. It is close to this point that the GR divides into two roads: the alternative route (see below) which goes via Aujols and the GR36 which goes down via Cavaniès in the Lot valley and climbs up again at Galessie. The two routes join up again at the hamlet of Mazuts.

The GR36 goes to the left along the Saint-Cirice road. At a cross, take the road on the right-hand side. In another 400 metres, go to the left down a paved track between oaks and hazel-nut trees as far as farm in the hamlet of Cavaniès. Go along a road which takes you to the D911 road. Cross the D911 and the railway. Keep straight on. At the edge of the River Lot go to the right along the old towpath. This takes you past a lock and then near a ruined mill. Go towards the right, then left on to a track which goes past some old gravel workings.

7Km
2

AUJOLS
Church with Romanesque belfry.

5Km
1:30

Old gravel working
Detour *10 mins*
ARCAMBAL
Towering over the village is a 15th-century château, still picturesque despite various revisions dating from several periods.

2Km
0:30

GALESSIE-BAS

Alternative route via Aujols to Mazuts. At the crossroads on the Saint-Cirice road, keep going eastwards on a tarmac track which lies straight ahead. Go to the right of a building and, in another 100 metres, go along to a track between low stone walls. Go down to Le Tréboulou stream. The path eventually emerges on to a wide cart track where you go left. This brings you to a road where you go left. Do not cross the bridge, but in another 100 metres, cross the stream by a paved track, which leads you to D49 road. Go along this to the right. In another 500 metres you come to a grove of oaks, go left along a grass path flanked with hedges. Some 250 metres further on, follow another path to the right up to a hill and skirt to the south of it. The track is flanked by a low wall. Further on, take another track heading north-east. You will come to a road where you turn to the right. This will take you to Aujols.

At the 'lake' go north between the mairie and the school. In another 500 metres you come to a crossroads, head right and take the second local footpath on the left, between two dry-stone walls. Stay on this track until you come to the D911 and cross it level with a quarry. Go up a pathway and cross the D49 road. Bear north-east and join the D49 again, turning to the right along it as far as a disused transformer. Go left and through the hamlet of Les Mazuts (map ref. b). This is the end of the alternative route.

Detour see left. Going straight on (east), crossing under the railway and then crossing the D911 road. Return to the GR36 the same way.

The GR36 returns to the edge of the River Lot. On reaching the foot of the cliff, go to the right along a pathway, cross the bridge over the railway and stay on the road as far as Galessie-Bas.

The GR follows the road towards Galessie-Haut for a short distance, then goes left on to a road leading to a water tower. Continue along a grass path. In another 600 metres, at the

3Km
1

Les Mazuts

(see map ref B)
To the south you can see the
waymarks of the alternative
GR36 route via Aujols.

3Km
0:45

crossroads, bear left on to a track up the hillside to the north of Pech Lougard. Farther on (IGN post 295) turn right (south-east), on to a stony track along the ridge. This brings you to the intersection of the D8 and D49, just before reaching the hamlet of Les Mazuts.

At the crossroads near the hamlet of Les Mazuts, the GR36 takes a short-cut to the north alongside a hedge, and then joins the D49. Follow this road, heading left, for some 50 metres. Then turn right, up a grassy track among trees. This track bends right and left before coming back to the D49, on which you head towards the right. In another 20 metres go up to the right on a paved track which overlooks the road. Before dropping down towards Béars you come to an intersection which is the junction of footpaths GR36 and GR46. To the north, GR46 goes down towards the River Lot and on towards Uzerche via Labastide-Murat and Rocamadour.

Najac

Junction of GR36 and GR46

The GR36 and GR46 share the same route towards the south-east as far as Beauregard, although waymarking refers to the GR36 only.

4Km
1

Detour, *30 mins*
VERS

Ⓗ 🏠 ⛺ 🍴 🚋 🚌

Follow the waymarked signs for the GR46, as it drops down to the village of Béars, crosses the River Lot and reaches Vers.

PASTURAT
🏠 ⛺

12Km
3

At the sign, the GR36 turns very sharply to the right and goes up to the TV relay station. It then crosses a plateau among box trees and junipers, continues along the cliff top to a paved track and goes on until it comes to a road. Turn left on to this. In another 300 metres go to the left at the crossroads, along the Pasturat road. A little further on go to the right along a track flanked with low walls and join a road, going left along it down to Pasturat.

The GR36 passes Pasturat church and then turns right (south-east) along the road to the bridge over the Lot. The camping site is on the opposite bank.

The GR footpath stays this side of the bridge, and continues along the river's edge. Another 700 metres further on, turn right and follow the path along the floor of a little valley and under a road bridge. In another 50 metres turn left up a pathway to the D10 road and turn right. In a few more metres, turn left, taking a paved track which heads south-east and passes through some trees. Further on, drop down into a little valley and up through an oak wood to the D8 road (north of the Mas de Parrot).

Take the D8 to the left for a short distance, then go left along a track running parallel to this road as far as a wayside cross. At that point veer left (northeast) down a track leading to the railway. Walk underneath the railway, turn right and follow the river Lot. Pass to the left of Port-la-Lèque farm and continue along the towpath overlooking the river. In another 400 metres keep along the edge of a field. Next take a road to the left. Some 600 metres farther on, continue along the track round the edge of a field and cross yet another field. In a fairly short distance you come to the towpath again. Pass a lock and come to a suspension bridge just outside Bouziès.

BOUZIÈS

(see map ref C)
On the other bank, at a place called the 'Défilé des Anglais', is a cavern which was fortified during the English occupation of the region early in the 13th century.

5Km
1:15

SAINT-CIRQ-LAPOPIE

Château, 16th century church with Romanesque sculpture

10Km
2:30

Junction with the GR 651 which goes via the Célé valley towards Béduer where it joins up with the GR65 (the *Saint James of Compostella* footpath, from Conques to Cahors).

The GR36 stays this side of the Bouziès suspension bridge, going east along the River Lot and under the railway bridge. Keep on the narrow, twisting towpath, which at one point is cut into the rock face. (On the opposite side is the confluence of the Lot and Célé rivers.)

Once past an old lock the path moves away from the foot of the cliff and brings you to a disused farm known as Ganil. Go around this to the road which skirts the foot of the cliff. Some 200 metres before reaching the houses, turn right on to a path which goes up to the Place de Sombral in Saint-Cirq-Lapopie.

In the village descend about 100 metres, turn right, pass the cemetery, cross the road opposite the oratory and go up the path called 'Chemin de Croix' to a chapel. Keep going to the plateau and follow the path heading south-south-west. At Lac Lapat continue due south to the crossroads (pond on the left). Keep going straight ahead on a path leading to a clearing. If walking from the opposite direction, when you arrive in this clearing go right, towards an enclosure, and keep the enclosure on your right. The footpath crosses the clearing and heads south-west along a track flanked with low walls. In another kilometre, take a road off to the left (heading south).

Beyond some crossroads, turn right at Cloup Cau on to a pebbly track down to the Bories Basses road. Cross the farm-yard and keep going along a track heading south-west. At the next intersection, the GR swings due south along a path which crosses a road. Keep heading in the same direction and going through some oak woods. When you come out of the woods, walk along fields and meadows till you come to a barn. From there a wide path heads south to a group of buildings called Mas de Janicou. Follow the waymarking to Concots.

Saint-Cirq-Lapopie

This medieval village perched on top of an enormous rocky escarpment, more than 100 metres above the left bank of the River Lot, is listed as a historical monument, and part of the surrounding area is registered as a site of outstanding beauty. The village is also a model of renovation (with no power and telephone cables or television aerials to be seen). Saint-Cirq-Lapopie was once the home of wood turners, copper smiths and craftsmen, and has since inspired painters and become a haven for artists. Strolling along the steep alleyways of the village, you will find old houses with overhanging upper storeys, exposed beams, half-timbering, towers, turrets, pointed Gothic windows, mullioned Renaissance bay-windows, lovely brown tiled roofs, and so on.

The châteaux which clung to this incredible rock face in the Middle Ages are now in ruins but if you follow the path upward to the top of the rock, you will be rewarded with a wonderful view. The wooded uplands on the edge of the Causse de Gramat stand out in relief; the Lot cuts down between the cliffs of Coudoulous, and winds around mixed arable farms; in the distance a road passes a little village built against the rock face.

There is a château to visit, the Gardette, below the church. This church and its lovely nave were built in the 16th century; its builder retained the remains of a Romanesque building and incorporated into it the Notre-Dame chapel. The ornamental bases of the columns and the capital with its carving of the implacable Judith, are among the finest examples of Romanesque sculpture.

Saint-Cirq

CONCOTS

(see map ref D)
Tower called 'Tour de l'Horloge'; pigeon house; turret; 'bolet'; outside staircase.

7Km
1:45

Take the D911 road towards Limogne. At the crossroads (wayside cross) go to the right along the Bach road. Ignore the Escabassole road which goes off to the left and in a short distance go left along a wide paved track. In another 2 kilometres you come to an intersection of four paths. Turn right and go on to a track between low walls (south-west). Beyond La Plante is another intersection (with a cross) where you turn left along a road and head south-east. Pass a well and a stone trough, keep going along the road for about another 100 metres and then turn left (east) on to a track with low walls. In another 500 metres go to the right (south) down a paved track leading to a house. Turn left (south-east) on to a track, (ignore the track and storage tank on the right) which brings you to the Mass Dégot intersection (height 301 metres).

Mas de Dégot

Mas de Dégot is the building that can be seen on the hills to the right. There is no sign here to tell you that you have met the GR65. To the right (south-west) it goes to Cahors (the Saint James of Compostella footpath from Conques to Cahors). To the left (north-east), the GR36 and GR65 share the same route as far as La Plane farm near Varaire.

4Km
1

Detour *15 mins*
BACH
✕ ♨

Detour
La Coste

The deserted hamlet of La Coste has houses in the Quercy style, with stone slab roof, bolet and soleilho — regional terms.

La Plane

At this point, the GR36 and GR65 separate. The GR65 turns north-east in the direction of Limogne, Cajarc and Figeac (the Saint James of Compostella footpath, from Conques to Cahors).

1Km
0:15

VARAIRE
⌂ ✕ ♓ ♨ ▭
(see map ref E)

At Mas de Dégot, the GR36 and GR65 turn left onto a wide track which begins as tarmac. Follow this as far as a gateway at one of the entrances to the Couanac hunting area. Turn right, along the fence and you cross a little valley where there is a well. Follow a track through trees which brings you to a wide paved track. A little further on, pass a track on the left and 300 metres further on there is a path on the left which goes to La Coste.

In another kilometre the GR footpaths reach the D52 road and some farm buildings at La Plane.

At La Plane the GR36 goes to the right along the D52 road. In another 250 metres turn left on to a tarmac track. This will bring you to the lake and church at Varaire.

The GR36 goes along the road to the right of Varaire church, passing the hamlet Puech du Lac. In another 200 metres turn right (south-east) on to a path flanked with low stone walls. This brings you to the Roman road from Cahors to Villefranche-de-Rouergue, and you go left along it. This meets the D52 road several times eventually becoming a path with hedges. Stay on it to the D53, then instead of crossing the road, head left along it for a few metres. Ignore a path going up to the left in a north-westerly direction and go straight ahead (north-east) on another track which goes close by a barn. In another 400 metres turn right on

to a path. This comes to a four-way inter-section after 200 metres. Drop down to the left and go by road to the Château de Marsa. Turn right and go along by the château wall, taking a stony path which goes down to a wash house. Go to the right of this and then up to the right on a grass path leading to the D53 road near a barn and wayside cross.

The GR36 continues left along the D53 to Beauregard.

8Km
2

Intersection

At this point, the GR36 and GR46 go separate ways. The GR46 goes south-east towards Saint-Antonin-Noble-Val and Cahuzac-sur-Vère.

This intersection is the starting point for the Tour des Gorges de l'Aveyron which follows the route of the GR 36 as far as Cahuzac-sur-Vère.

BEAUREGARD

✗ ⚖ ☷

In the square, outside the church with Romanesque carvings is a 15th-century cross. Old market buildings. House in rural style with a stone roof supported on a 'tas-de-charge' — massive stone seat or cushion.

Beyond the village the GR36 leaves the D53 by the first path on the right, which bears to the left down to a stream. Cross the stream by a little bridge. Go up the path, taking the first track on the left. Cross another track and then the D55. Keep going along a sunken lane. As you draw level with a wayside cross you intersect the D24. Keep straight on along a road. In another 150 metres, at Patras, go right (north-east) along a grass path. Further on take a path suitable for motor vehicles. Follow it for 100 metres, and at the next intersection turn left (north-east) along a stony track between low walls.

10Km
2:30

In another 1.5 kilometres (height 353 metres, map ref F) the GR footpath heads to the right (south-east) along a wide paved path. At Falgayras (IGN height 363 metres) turn left and in another 50 metres turn right on to a path which takes you to the D55. Take this road in a southerly direction, pass an ancient priory and go into Laramière.

LARAMIÈRE

Priory of Notre-Dame de
Laramière is a dependency
of the abbey at La Couronne
near Angoulême constructed
by Augustinian order in 12th
century. Still in existence are
the chapel with Romanesque
substructures, the chapter
house and the tithe barn. A
key stone in a loft has been
decorated with the hand of
God the Father, bestower of
blessings.

5Km
1:15

The GR36 leaves by the D55 road heading east. Beyond the village, follow a track to the left (north-east). Further on take the Vialars road to the right. Beyond this little place head right, in the direction of Le Mazet, then take the first track to the left, under a high-tension wire, to the hamlet of Le Puech.

Le Puech

The GR footpath crosses the D76 and turns left (north-east) on to the old Villefranche road, which skirts the boundary wall of the Loc-Dieu estate. Further on, stay on the road. Beyond a saw mill turn right and enter Savignac.

Detour 15 mins
Abbey of Loc-Dieu

Locus Dei, the place of God.
Cistercian abbey of
Bernardins, founded in 1123,
sacked and burned by the
English in the 15th century,
then restored in the 16th
century. Became a private
estate during the Revolution
and was sold to the Cibiel
family in 1812. Romanesque
church and cloister. Hiding
place of Leonardo da Vinci's
La Gioconda (Mona Lisa)
during the Occupation. Open
to the public.

4Km
1

Detour see left. Take the D76 to the right and D115 to the left heading in an easterly direction.

SAVIGNAC

(see map ref G)
15th-century church, twin
bell towers with pinnacle
turrets. Spring with
underground basin.

6Km
1:30

The GR36 passes Savignac church and heads south-east along the Coustels road crossing the D926. Keep straight ahead down a wide track, crossing Malpas stream. Beyond La Teule farm the track becomes a road which swings north-east. Pass Le Mas de Bonnet and then Beauregard agricultural college. Drop down to the D911 road, joining it in Villefranche-de-Rouergue.

VILLEFRANCHE-DE-ROUERGUE

(see map ref H)
*The Pearl of the Rouergue.
Ancient fortified town built on
orders of Alphonse de
Poitiers, brother of French
king Saint-Louis. The
Romans were attracted by
the silver mines in the area;
an inscription in one of the
underground galleries
proves that they were
working the lode during the
reign of Tiberius.
Visit the 12th-century
collegiate church; the 15th-
century Charterhouse of
Saint-Sauveur; the
17th-century Chapelle des
Pénitents noirs; modern
Chapelle de la Sainte*

14Km
3:30

The GR36 leaves Villefranche heading south-west via the D47. Turn left on to the track which passes by the stadium, the camping site and the River Aveyron. At the industrial park head towards the right along the D89. In another 500 metres, beyond a bridge, go to the left up a track to the plateau and cross the D89. Keep heading towards the south-west along a track. At the next intersection turn left (south) and take the D89 to the right for 100 metres. Where it intersects with the D115 road (height 364 metres) go towards the south-west on a track which goes near to the Mas de Jammes. Go to the left past the Mas de Jammes and further on, at a fork, take the left-hand track (south-east) across the Causse de Souzils. Walk between a 'cazelle' (little dry-stone building) and a ruined building. At the next crossroads (near the hamlet of Laumière) turn right (south-west). In another kilometre go left (due south) on to a track which eventually becomes a pathway between stone walls. Cross a road and keep straight on past kilometre post 385. Cross another road. Not far

Mining in the Gorges de l'Aveyron

Between Villefranche-de-Rouergue and Laguépie lies an area with about 30 ore veins mainly containing silver-bearing lead and copper. These began to be exploited in Gallo-Roman times (Villefranche — Najac). In the 13th century, the consular accounts of Najac mentioned mines in the locality. At Saint-Antonin and Figeac, and later at Villefranche between 1300 and 1556, royal mints were operating with metal from the region. A manuscript tells us that in the 16th century, German specialists discovered veins at Courbières and Najac 'after discovering the vein of silver they poured 6,000 pounds of ingots'. Prospecting was carried out under the orders of Colbert and Louis XIV, resulting in mining operations at Villefranche, Najac and Laguépie.

The mines in the region declined during the Revolution and under the Empire, not reviving until the Industrial Revolution in the middle of the 19th century. Only the shallow coal seams at La Salvetat des Carts (near Najac) and at Puech Mignon (near Laguépie) were prospected, but claims were granted in 1840 and 1850 in the Puechiguier region (Serène valley) where veins of copper and silver-bearing lead are to be found. Because of the mining, the railway came to the Aveyron Gorges. Other mine workings were opened at Farguerolles (Monteils), Le Bastit, Lespagne and Najac railway station. In the face of competition from more productive foreign mines work ceased in 1879 and 1904 at La Baume and La Maladrerie (Villefranche-de-Rouergue). Towards the end of the Second World War, the Germans, who were short of copper, gave orders for mining operations to begin beneath Cassagnes (Najac).

Famille. Stroll in ancient streets with old houses, and in arcaded Place Notre Dame.
Starting point for the GR62b to Rodez.

MONTEILS

🏠 ⌂ ⚠ ✕ 🏛 🚂 ℹ

(see map ref I)
About 7 kilometres from Najac and 12 kilometres from Villefranche-de-Rouergue, on banks of Aveyron. Charming little place with rich past.
The new church was built between 1863 and 1866, acting as a focal point for a working population whose family names revealed, in the local dialect, their main occupation. For examples, 'Del Pech' or 'Del Causse' reflected the location of the land on which they worked. 'Vernhes' was the name given to those who dyed cloth with rushes, willow and alder. People were needed to tend the vines, and especially to tread the grapes at harvest — they were called 'Calcat'.
On this walk, you cross a railway bridge over the Capdenac-Toulouse line which was constructed between 1854 and 1858, needing nine bridges and nine tunnels for the travelling between Monteils and Najac. In an area near an oak road you will see remains of ovens which were used during the war for making charcoal.

8Km
2

beyond the Maison de la Carcine, at a grassy patch, go left down the pathway to the Dominican convent of Monteils. Road number D47 will take you to the centre of Monteils.

The GR36 leaves Monteils heading southwest, crosses a loop in the D47 road and climbs through woods to the foot of the Puech de la Borde (height 474 metres, view) passing the farm of the same name. Go on in a southerly direction and cross the D47. At the crossroads (Cross of Man) follow the road round the Puech de Miremont to the east and along the ridge to Courbières hamlet. At the hairpin bend leave the road to the 13th century château and go straight ahead (west) down a track which crosses a stream. The footpath turns left along the bank and then to the right alongside the Aveyron. You now come to the railway bridge on the Capdenac-Toulouse line. Pedestrians may use as a concession from the SNCF; please do not loiter.

The GR36 crosses the bridge, going parallel to the railway track. At the far end of the bridge turn left, walk under the bridge and follow the left bank of the Aveyron. Further on, near a spring, the GR leaves the river and climbs up to a pass in a cutting. From here, via an oak wood, you are overlooking a wide sweep of the Aveyron. Beyond a stream turn and take the right-hand path. The route passes by some old slate quarries and a spring, coming eventually to the Rue de l'Hiversenc. Take the alleyways to the main square in Najac.

MONTEILS

🏠 ⌂ 🛖 🍴 🚉 📮 🅿

(see map ref I)

Alternative route Monteils to Loze via GR de Pays.

This route, waymarked in yellow and red, makes it possible to go on a circular tour of 74 kilometres beginning and ending in Monteils. It uses the following routes: GR de Pays, Monteils to Loze; GR46, Loze to Beauregard; GR36, Beauregard to Monteils.

Take the D514 road north-west. About 500 metres beyond the village, turn right on to a road leading to the Fontaliès. From the hamlet, go left along the track beside the Assou river. At the far end you will find there is a gap in the waymarking. When you come to the hut go to the left and across the bridge over the stream, walk along a field, cross the footbridge over another stream and follow the D514 to the right.

You are now entering Tarn-et-Garonne. At the crossroads take the left-hand road, D75 for a few metres then go left on to a track which winds upwards to the Pech de Mourtayrol and rejoins the D75. Go left along the road to Castenet where there are guest rooms.

17Km
4:15

From the village go up to the left (east). At a wayside cross turn right (south-west) up a pathway to a bend in the road. From there, go straight ahead to the Pech, then come down (north-west) to the Pech de Gary. Keep going in the same direction to the crossroads near Caussanel. From there take the road to the left, cross the next bend and then the bridge over Ferran stream and turn right on to a pathway to the Mas de Maillet. Further on, go to the left of Cambayrac hamlet. Follow the road south-west, cross the D84 and go on along a pathway to a little place called Causseviel. At the old church, go along the road to the right for 300 metres, and then take the track which continues the line of the road. The path turns left, heading west. Follow the waymarking carefully through the woods, as there are many changes of direction. You will eventually arrive at the hamlet of La Rabarie (see map ref A).

From La Rabarie the GR takes the road north. This side of the crossroads (spot height 359)

follow a track to the left which is low-lying, and takes you past many springs, until it comes out eventually onto the D84 road. Follow the road to the left and enter the camping site. Go to the left around the pond and at the far end go up a pathway through a wood. Then take a road to the right which will bring you to Parisot.

PARISOT

🏕 ✕ 🚂 🚌

If you climb the steps to the top of Parisot's park, you will have a commanding view over the countryside.

8.5Km
2:15

From the Place de la Mairie, go to the south and round past the church. On the outskirts, turn right along a pathway between hedges and right again on the road to Roux farm. At the next farm, cross the D926 road and take the Majac road (north-west). In another 500 metres go to the left along the track leading to Les Boules. Once there, turn right (north-west). In another 700 metres take the right-hand fork (north) and go along the road to the right, coming to Majac.

In Majac turn left (north-west). Go down via a farm road, which eventually becomes a path, and cross a stream. In very wet weather, at this point, several metres of the path could be under water. The GR goes left along the D97 road for a distance, then goes up to the right by a short, steep path winding between hedges. At the ruined chapel of Saint-Caprais, follow the track between low stone walls and go down into the Bonnette valley. This brings you out at a bend on the D97. Cross the bridge over the river, continue south for 200 metres and then, opposite La Luzette mill, go up a steep sloping path to Loze.

Parisot

Near the surrounding walls is the magnificent Saint-Andéol church. The church treasures include a gem-encrusted 14th-century silver-on-walnut processional cross, decorated with scrolls and 15th-century enamel additions; two 18th-century silver chalices; and an 18th-century gilded wooden statue of the Virgin and Child. Outside the walls, on the southern side of the village, is the 15th-century Château de Lastorguidé. Further on is the Porte Genebrière, and the 16th-century market building which dates from the Middle Ages. In the plain below the village, overlooking the Seye valley, are the ruins of the Château de Labro; the château was the birthplace of Jean de la Valette, Grand Master of the Knights of Malta, who defeated Suleiman the Magnificent.

Parisot has a magnificent man-made lake which was opened to the public in the summer of 1973 and is mainly used for water sports. The very popular farm market is held in the village on the second Friday in the month.

NAJAC

🏠 ⌂ ⛺ 🍴 🚂 🚌 🚆 ℹ️

*Ancient stronghold of the
Counts of Toulouse.
Château dating from the 12th
and 13th centuries built by
Alphonse de Poitiers,
brother of French king Saint-
Louis. Thirteenth-century
church, the oldest Gothic
religious building in
Rouergue. Arcaded houses.
Springs, one of which is in
monolithic granite. Craft
centre.*

**6Km
1:30**

MERGIEUX
⛺

*(see map ref J)
Hamlet perched on a ridge
between the River Aveyron
and the Loubezac stream.*

**7Km
1:45**

LAGUÉPIE

🏠 ⛺ 🍴 🚂 🚌 🚆 ℹ️

*The first chateau at Laguépie
was destroyed during the
crusades in 1211 and 1216
of Simon de Montfort. Since
then Laguépie has been the
scene of many battles. The
chateau was rebuilt and then
destroyed again after the
Revolution.*

The GR footpath leaves Najac heading west along the road below the church. At a secluded house, go left along the old paved Gallo-Roman road leading to the 13th-century Pont Saint-Blaise bridge. Cross the bridge, turn left and follow the Aveyron to Cantagrel. On the very outskirts go up to the right through some woods to the hamlet of Bastit. Follow the road from there heading south-west. At an electricity transformer, go left (south-east) down a track to La Gasquié. Turn right (west), head for a stream, cross it, and then go down a track along the right bank. At the second intersection take the path up to the VVF (Village Vacances Famille) camping site at Mergieux.

Head east from the camping site at Mergieux, round the spur on the forest drive which drops down towards the Aveyron. Walk under the railway viaduct and cross the Loubezac stream. Between the river and the sheer cliffs, take a pathway among some box trees. This emerges in some plantations of poplars, and you then take a culvert across the Puech Meja stream, the boundary between Aveyron and Tarn-et-Garonne. The footpath continues along the road to the old mill of Saint-Cambraire. Walk under a railway bridge and take a cement road to the camping site and naval base at Laguépie. Turn right before the bridge and go along the side of a little square, then go left along a little sunken section. Via the Avenue de la Gare, cross the Aveyron and go into Laguépie.

The GR36 leaves Laguépie by the bridge across the Viaur and enters Saint-Martin-Laguépie. This is the starting point for the GR de Pays which goes to the east towards Tanus. The GR36 goes to the right along the D9 road, and not much further on turns left up a pathway to the château. Continuing in a southerly direction, go along a stream and then cross it. Follow the road for another kilometre and cross the D34 road. On this part of the walk you will have very good views of the surrounding area.

10Km
2:30

Cordes

On the road for La Gasquié, go down the first track on the left, cross some enclosed fields and go across a bridge over the Aymer stream. Go up a wide paved track and turn left off it in a short distance. The GR footpath crosses a wood and passes Tibourlat farm. Keep straight on at the crossroads (spot height 278). This side of La Vergne farm turn right (south-west) on to a path leading to Puech Gaubil (see map ref k). At the Puech Gaubil transformer the footpath turns left and follows the road for some 250 metres. At the intersection, go almost straight across and turn right on to a track leading to Puech Gax (cross). Follow the road to the right for 600 metres and then leave it, taking a track to the left (view over the Château de Boisse). Take the road which goes close to La Plaine farm. In another 200 metres, go right (south-west) on to a pathway which goes down past a vineyard. Lower down, go left along the D30 road, cross the bridge over the Cérou and enter Les Cabannes.

LES CABANNES
△ ♟

At this point the GR36 connects with the GR de Pays. Its yellow-red waymarkers lead west towards Penne.

1Km
0:15

Detour *45 mins*
LA VÉDILLERIE
⌂

CORDES
🏨 △ ✕ 🚉 🚍 🚃 🛈

Medieval town founded in 1222 by Count Raymond VII of Toulouse and named after the Spanish city of Cordoba (Cordoue in French). Many strongholds in the south-west bear the name of a Spanish or Italian city. Clamber up the very steep streets to Cordes-le-Haut. Medieval old town; Gothic houses with carvings. The once prosperous industries of tanning and embroidery have been perpetuated throughout the years by large numbers of craftsmen.

Bégoutte
(see map ref L)
The millstone caverns of Bégoutte may be visited by arrangement with the Mayor of Amarens. These deep, rugged cavities were hollowed out by hand to fashion the millstones which ground the grain of southern France up to the end of the 19th century. The Bégoutte millstone cavern is 100 metres long, 35 metres wide and 14 metres high. The annual wine festival is held in this immense hall every summer.

15Km
4

Go right along the D91 to the 'Pont des Aries' which crosses the Cérou. Cross over the bridge and just beyond the mill at La Bogne go right along the D7. Take a pathway on your left into the Cérou valley. Follow the path to the right where it joins a road, turn left for 100 metres and you arrive at La Védillerie.

In Les Cabannes, near an ironmonger's, the GR36 crosses the D91 road and goes straight ahead (south-east) up a road to Cordes.

From Cordes cemetery, the GR36 takes the track down to La Devèze heading south-west. Stay on the road and then take a pathway leading to Les Crozes. At the intersection, ignore the yellow and red waymarkings on the right, which refer to the local footpath, GR du Pays, for Penne.

From Les Crozes the GR36 goes to the right (south-west) and up to the plateau, passing to the left of Malbousquet. Cross a road (spot height 291) and go down through scrub heading south-east and crossing the D25 road. Cross a stream. Near the next railway bridge, turn right. Walk under the second bridge. Beyond it, on the right, is a pathway leading to Bégoutte.

Beyond Bégoutte, the GR footpath continues along the road (south-east), crosses a stream and takes a short cut to Saint-André abbey. In another 350 metres, turn left (south-east) on to a pathway which takes you to Bois-Redon. Just past this hamlet, head down the track which goes south-west and then south to a tarmac track. Go along it for some metres and then head south-west along a pathway beside a stream, coming to a bridge north of Lintin.

Cross this bridge, turn right (south-west) and follow a track alongside Saint-Hussou stream. This brings you to Le Cayla.

Le Cayla

*Oldest part of château dates
from the 15th century.
Several vaults have key
stones dated 1768 or 1769.
The château grounds were
the property of the Guérin
family; their ancestors came
from Auvergne and
Rouergue and can be traced
back to the 9th century. Now
famous because two people,
Eugénie and Maurice,
became poets. Imbued with
a feeling for nature by her
surroundings, Eugénie wrote
her 'Journal' and copious
correspondence. Maurice
wrote magnificent prose
poems which George Sand
brought to the attention of
the world in 1840.*

CAHUZAC-SUR-VÈRE

(see map ref M)

7Km
1:45

Coustous

*This is is the starting point
for the local footpath (GR de
Pays), waymarked in yellow
and red, which leads to
Penne.*

2Km
0:30

The GR36 takes the road on the left heading
south-east. At Cinq Peyres, go to the right (due
south) and take the first pathway on the right
leading to the cemetery and then the village of
Cahuzac-sur-Vère.

The waymarking for the GR36 stops here.
There are several ways in which walkers can
travel to Albi, where the GR36 is waymarked
once more as far as Canigou:
1. Take the train from Cahuzac-sur-veère halt
   (trains are infrequent).
2. Walk to the station at Tessonières (10 km of
   unwaymarked footpath via Senouillac).
3. Continue south-west on the GR46, joining a
   GR de Pays (local footpath) to Lisle-sur-
   Tarn (frequent trains for Albi and Toulouse).

The GR46 heads south-west along an alleyway
below the village. Turn off this alleyway on to a
track and cross a stream. At Planolles farm go
right. In a short distance (spot height 227) take
a paved track on the left. Further on, bear to
the right along the D26 road heading north. At
an intersection where there is a cross, turn left
(west) to Les Garrigues farm and take a paved
track to the hamlet of Vernus. From there,
continue along a road (south-west) to an
intersection on the D15. Cross over to the
tarmac track opposite, which passes a spring.
Cross the bridge over La Mouline stream, and
just beyond, turn right on to a pathway beside
the stream. The GR footpath comes to the
Coustous farm.

From Coustous farm, the GR46 continues
westwards along the edge of the stream. In
another 600 metres turn left (south-west) along
a cart track which crosses another stream.
Coming to Pradet, cross a road and go up a
grass track to the village of Castelnau-de-
Montmiral.

Castelnau-de-Montmiral

The very name Castelnau-de-Montmiral (Castellum novum montis mirabilis: new castle on a hill with a view) tells all about the purpose of this location. Firmly seated on a rock jutting out over the Vère valley, the protecting ramparts of this medieval stronghold could easily oversee the comings and goings of any 'undesirables', from whichever direction they cared to approach. The Albigensian Crusade, the Hundred Years War and the Wars of Religion have all played a part in its eventful past.

The streets still show noticeable signs of the distant past: the Porte des Garrics, circa 1300; Tour de Toulouse, 1620, overlooking the valley; Place des Arcades, with two buildings dated 1630 and 1634. In the Rue Basse notice a very old house, and the splendid Renaissance door which survives from a convent formerly on the site, as well as the surviving parts of the Maison Tonnac in the Place de la Rose. The Tour de l'Hôpital overlooks the former royal road from La Lèbre to Gaillac and provides views to Le Verdier, Vieux and even, in clear weather, the belfry at Cordes. The Rue des Chiffonniers contains a Renaissance house.

CASTELNAU-DE-MONTMIRAL
✗ ≞ 🛈
(see map ref N)

7Km
1:45

From the south of Castelnau the GR46 crosses the D964 road and continues along the road opposite. In a bend, carry straight on along a grass path leading to Les Mazières farm. Turn left past Les Dumasses. Further on, take a road to the right (north-west). In another 350 metres go left (south-west) on to a pathway. This leads to the D5 road, where you turn right and walk along it. When the two roads fork (spot height 286), go along a track heading west at first and then north-west, passing close by the ruins of Château de Lagarde. Dropping down towards the Vère valley you then go left on to the road for Brugnac.

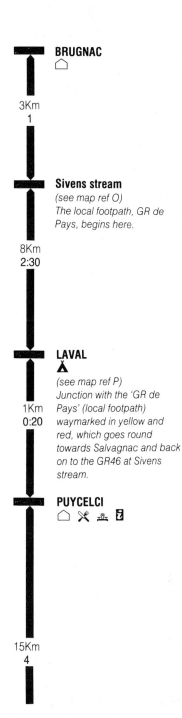

BRUGNAC

3Km
1

Sivens stream
(see map ref O)
The local footpath, GR de
Pays, begins here.

8Km
2:30

LAVAL
(see map ref P)
Junction with the 'GR de
Pays' (local footpath)
waymarked in yellow and
red, which goes round
towards Salvagnac and back
on to the GR46 at Sivens
stream.

1Km
0:20

PUYCELCI

15Km
4

Before reaching Brugnac, near a wayside cross, the GR46 turns left. In another 300 metres go to the right along a sunken track as far as Meilhou farm. From there go down, cross the Combe-Escure stream and turn right. The route then changes direction several times. Cross the D32 road and head for Les Ramadiesses. Before reaching the farm go left and down towards the stream.

The GR46 goes along the left bank of Sivens stream and as it leaves the wood, turns left (south-west) up to the ridge. At the Planettes farm go downwards to the right (north), cross Pradel stream and take the road to Lacapelle. From the cemetery take the track which goes down and across Colombier stream, then go up to Frayssine. Head west. In another kilometre go to the right, down a pathway (north-west and then north), crossing Rieubois stream. On arriving at Ligounié take a path down to a little place called Laval.

From Laval the GR46 goes northwards on the road across the Vère, crosses the D664 road and takes a steep path up to Puycelci.

From Porte Hirissou at Puycelci, the GR46 goes alongside the ramparts and due north down to Le Roc farm. To the right of the farm, head towards Audoulou stream and take the little bridge across it. The footpath climbs the hillside opposite and enters Grésigne State Forest (see page 149).

Near a ruined hut, GR 46 turns along a pathway heading left. Turn right at an intersection (north-east) on to the forest road to La Plégade roundabout. Some 2 kilometres north of there, take the first forest trail on the left. In a bend, cross the ditch on the left and go up a pathway (north-west) to Perilhac forester's

Circular tour

This circular tour links Lisle-sur-Tarn (which has a good train service on the Toulouse to Albi line) and Sivens forest, which is on the route of footpath GR46. Two walking tours are possible from Lisle-sur-Tarn:

One-day walk (25 kilometre circular tour) via La Jasse de Sivens;
Fifty-kilometre walk via the GR de Pays as far as La Jasse and Sivens stream, footpath GR46 to Laval, and return via the GR de Pays from Laval to Montarels, then Saint-Salvy-de-Coutens.

Alternative For the walker on the GR46 route this circular tour can also be undertaken from Sivens stream or Laval (see pages 141 and 144) by following the local footpath, GR de Pays, to the crossroads near Le Tescon stream, through Les Montarels to Lisle-sur-Tarn, returning by way of Montaigut and La Jasse.

LISLE-SUR-TARN

(see map ref g)
Stronghold dating from 1229; terraced gardens overlooking the Tarn; former port on the Tarn connected with the Gaillac wine trade; Raymond Lafage Museum, drawings and paintings from the 17th and 19th centuries; Gallo-Roman objects discovered at the turn of the century on the site of Montans, including wine pottery; buildings which overhang the street.

9Km
2:30

Montaigut

Site surrounded by earthworks (ancient defensive ditches); church dating from the 11th and 12th centuries; the original site of Lisle-sur-Tarn village, levelled in 1229.

Waymarking for the GR de Pays begins by lake Lisle-sur-Tarn, 1 kilometre to the north-east of the town, at Le Pujol. Cross the N88 road. Beyond the level crossing take the first road on the left (sign for Saint-Vincent). Then go along the first dirt path on the right, between fields and vines. At the next intersection turn left (south-west). Further on, at the second intersection, turn right towards Oursou. Before reaching the farm, go to the right along a track to the Mazou estate. Cross the D18 road, then go across a tarmac track near a wayside cross and up to the cemetery and the church at Montaigut (shown on the IGN map as Montégut).

From Montaigut the GR goes down to the right of the cemetery alongside the vineyard. Cross a road and a little further on turn right (north-west) towards Les Alberts. There turn left along a track which goes around the highest part of the hill and into the woods.

At the next fork, this side of Loubersac, you can join the return leg of the circular tour by going down to the left — this is shown as a dotted line and marked Hors GR on the map. The GR footpath carries straight on, passes close to Loubersac, crosses Rabistau stream and goes up to the hamlet of Saint-Etienne-de-Vionan.

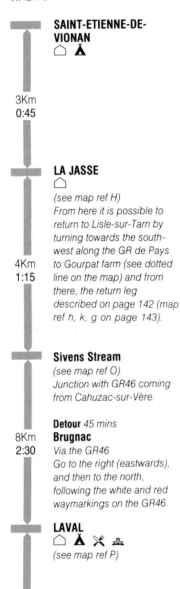

SAINT-ETIENNE-DE-VIONAN

3Km
0:45

At the wayside cross of Saint-Etienne-de-Vionan the GR footpath goes to the left of the church and takes the road northwards to the D99 road. Go straight across the D99 and take a track heading north-west through woods and hedgerows. Cross Tescou stream and go ahead (north-west) into the forest of Sivens, walking alongside a nursery plantation. This brings you to the track leading to the clearing at La Jasse.

LA JASSE

4Km
1:15

(see map ref H)
From here it is possible to return to Lisle-sur-Tarn by turning towards the south-west along the GR de Pays to Gourpat farm (see dotted line on the map) and from there, the return leg described on page 142 (map ref h, k, g on page 143).

To carry on with the circular tour in the direction of Laval, leave the forest road and take the first track on the left (north-west). At Clot de Mouysset at the next crossroads take a pathway on the left going down into a small valley. Then the path climbs to an area cleared of trees. Further on, the GR crosses a stream and heads north climbing to join the D5 road (see map ref i). Take the D5 heading left (west) for some metres, then turn right and go along between some oak trees. The GR footpath goes down towards the north-east, then northwards, and arrives at Sivens Stream.

Sivens Stream

(see map ref O)
Junction with GR46 coming from Cahuzac-sur-Vère.

From Sivens stream follow the white and red waymarkings on the GR46 towards the north-west (see description on page 141) to Laval.

Detour *45 mins*

8Km
2:30

Brugnac
Via the GR46
Go to the right (eastwards), and then to the north, following the white and red waymarkings on the GR46.

LAVAL

(see map ref P)

The circular tour now starts the return leg towards Lisle-sur-Tarn. Leave the GR46 which heads north towards Puycelci. From Laval follow the yellow and red waymarkings of the GR de Pays. Take the D1 road for 500 metres towards the south-west. At the bend, turn left on to a pathway up through the woods. Cross a road (spot height 274) and come to Pechnarier farm. Go down along a wide, snaking path, ford the Granges stream and walk up to Le Bragard. From there, follow the D20 road to the left (south-east). In another

10Km
2:45

700 metres go to the right, along a paved track. Go well to the left of the chapel of Saint-Julien. Cross Le Tescounet stream, then turn left past the chestnut grove. At the corner of this grove, go to the right (south-south-west) up a path which is tarmac by the time you reach Polonis farm. Turn left on to the D5 road which takes you to Clayrac.

Opposite the access road to Clayrac farm, the GR goes to the right in a southerly direction, then swings south-west before crossing a road at Les Condats. Further on, pass the houses at Les Michous and continue south-west to a crossroad.

Crossroads near Le Tescou Stream
(see map ref J)

The footpath GR de Pays does not cross the stream at the crossroads, but heads east along the 'old Montauban road'. Cross the D28 road, carry on to another road and go along it to the right. Just before the bridge across Le Tescou stream, turn to the left along a track leading to Le Fraysse. From this point keep heading east, cross two roads and you arrive at Les Montarels.

6Km
1:30

Detour *15 mins*
SALVAGNAC
🏠 Å ✕ ⚓ 🛈
Carry straight on (south-south-east) along the road which crosses Le Tescou stream.

Salvagnac
The town is built on a rocky crag which was inhabited in the distant past by a Gaulish clan of the Volces Tectosages tribe known as the Tasconi. Here they built their huts of clay daub and thatch. Their clan name has survived in the name of Le Tescou stream.

Salvagnac has retained some signs of its medieval past, in the form of two towers of its feudal château. Memories of its military past are preserved in the rusty, blackened 10-pound cannon-ball still embedded in the stonework of the north tower.

Besides the cannon-ball, at Notre-Dame-de-Salvagnac there is a small museum of sacred art objects, including among other things a collection of Apostles carved in wood inlaid with pure gold, and a statue of the Virgin and Child sculpted from a single block.

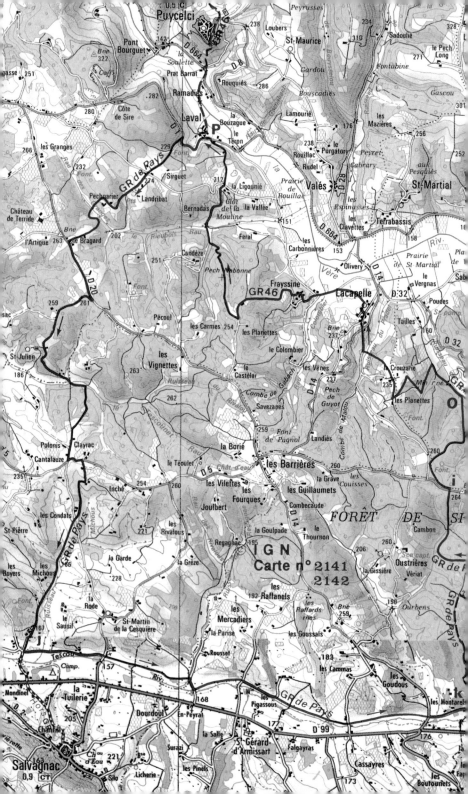

Les Montarels
(see map ref K)

4Km
1

Tumulus of Saint-Salvy

Viewing point over the vineyards and plain of the Tarn. The tumulus has a cross at the top raised by a Catholic mission in 1899.

6Km
1:30

LISLE-SUR-TARN
🏠 ⛺ ✕ 🚂 🚌 ℹ

(see map ref g)
Stronghold dating from 1229; terraced gardens overlooking the Tarn; former port on the Tarn connected with the Gaillac wine trade; Raymond Lafage Museum, drawings and paintings from the 17th and 19th centuries.

At the next intersection, the GR de Pays divides into two: left (north) you can continue via Le Gourpat farm and the forester's lodge at La Jasse, and from there rejoin the GR46 at Sivens stream (see dotted line on map) right (south) continues towards Lisle-sur-Tarn (see description below).

Just beyond Les Montarels, turn right and cross Le Tescou stream, take the D99 road left for 100 metres and then go up to the right in the direction of La Muscadelle. At the intersection near Coudougnac, go left and then right, between two vineyards, towards Le Cayla. A short distance before the reservoir turn left and then right, down a pathway which crosses Rabistau stream. Next walk up to Belle-Viste and turn right, taking a tarmac track. In another 500 metres turn right again along a path which takes you through vineyards to an ancient burial mound.

The GR footpath continues down a pathway (south), turns left, then right and enters the hamlet of Saint-Salvy (shown as Louvignes on the IGN map). Cross the D18 road to Bernis where there is a 300-year old oak. In another 50 metres turn left (south-east) to Oursou. From there, rejoin the 'outward' leg of the tour, eventually crossing the railway, then the N88 road, and arriving back at Lisle-sur-Tarn lake. The waymarking ends there. A little road heading south-west brings you to the centre of Lisle-sur-Tarn.

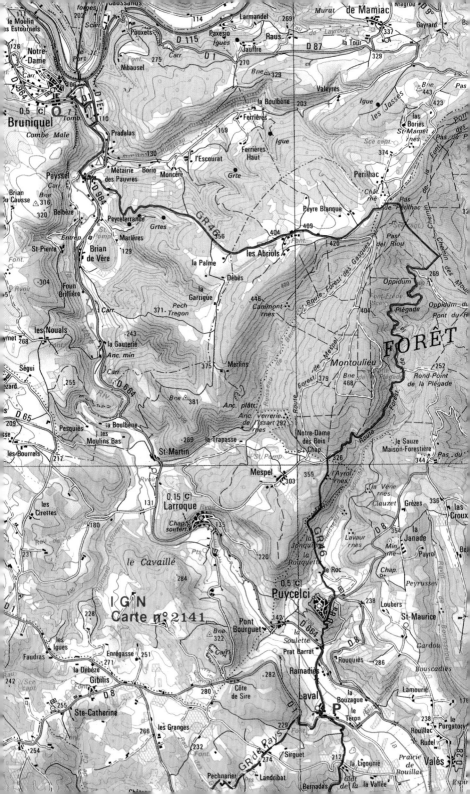

lodge, where the GR footpath leaves the State Forest. The footpath goes left (southwest) on to the road for Abriols. From this little hamlet a track leads to the right (west-northwest) and down to the tiny village of Payssel. Cross over the D964 road, take the footbridge across the Vère, turn right and walk along the left bank. In another 800 metres cross over the bridge and turn immediately left down the embankment on to a path along the right bank. At another bridge, cross the Vère again and walk along the D1 road. The GR footpath comes out near the wash house at Bruniquel.

Grésigne Forest

Grésigne Forest covers a huge area between Bruniquel, Puycelci, Castelnau, Saint-Beauzile, Penne and Vaour. It has been a State Forest since the time of Louis XIV. At the present time forestry is the only activity there, but it has known some very eventful times. It may well have been inhabited in prehistoric times, although the only remains (dolmens, menhir, caverns, tombs, etc.) are to be found around the edges. From historical times there are a scattering of oppida and camps at places such as Caillaret, Saint-Clément, La Baronde, Pont du Renard, Tour de Métal, Montagudet, La Plégade.

Then there are Roman roads and megaliths at La Peyro Signado. The are 15 sites of former glassworks which, during the 12th and 13th centuries, provided a livelihood for many people in Grésigne. There are many charcoal-burners' sites. For a long time the forest was the prime energy source for all industries in the surrounding region, particularly the foundries at Bruniquel and Puycelci.

Traces of all this industry can still be seen in the form of specially constructed water sources and furnaces.

BRUNIQUEL

(see map ref Q)

9Km
2:40

The GR46 goes down from the foot of Bruniquel village. Cross the Vère and take the bridge across the Aveyron. Go left for 50 metres, cross a ditch and take a steep path towards the north. At Gautier farm turn right and go up on to the high ground. Take a wide track to the north-east for 400 metres. At the bend go straight ahead along a grass path between two walls. At the three-way inter-section take the right-hand track (east) towards Moncéré. Before reaching this little hamlet turn right and continue eastwards through the scrub, passing to the south of the

Puech (spot height 303). Further on take a paved track to the right. Take the D33 road to the right for 200 metres, then go down and to the right for L'Ermitage farm. Cross the river Aveyron, then the D115 road, and arrive at Penne.

Bruniquel

According to local tradition, the village was founded in the 6th century by Queen Brunehaut, daughter of the Visigoth King Athanagilde, and the village was named after her. Legend has it that Clotaire, son of her rival Frédégonde, seized the Queen and had her executed by tying her to the tail of a wild horse. This took place at a spot on the edge of the village known ever since as *Côte Rouge* (Red Hill). It is said that prior to her execution, she was imprisoned in one of the château's towers.

Today's historian sees in the name a diminutive of Brunic, itself derived from the Germanic root Berno. Bruniquel was a trading town, reaching its highest point in the Middle Ages before beginning a slow decline following the Revocation of the Edict of Nantes (1685) — a law which granted religious and civil liberties to French Protestants, promulgated by Henry IV in 1598 and revoked by Louis XIV in 1685. Over 800 inhabitants of Bruniquel chose exile rather than compromise their consciences.

Two châteaux overlook the valley, the *castel biel* of the 13th and 14th centuries and the *castel djoubé*, 1485-1510, subsequently altered many times, even as late as the 18th century. Crouching alongside them, the 'old village' occupies the northern part of the town. It has preserved its ancient dwellings (mostly from the 15th, 16th and 17th centuries) and its narrow streets with evocative names such as Rue Droite, Rue Bombe-Cul, Rue Trotte-Garce and so on. There are also traces of the two sets of encircling walls in which there used to be seven gates, some of which have survived to the present day.

PENNE

(see map ref B)

3Km
0:45

Alternative route Penne to Cordes via GR ɑe Pays. This route makes it possible to go on a circular tour of 76 kilometres beginning and ending in Penne.

As far as Pech Grignal the footpath follows the same route as GR46 (see page 160).

A Romantic Legend

Penne is an important feature of the Albigeois region on the Quercy boundary, and was long seen as the key to the Aveyron valley. It has been occupied since early times, as is proved by finds of Gaulish and Roman coins. The village has scarcely altered in size since the Middle Ages, and is overlooked by the ruins of a 12th-century feudal château perched on an amazing rocky crag. The site could hardly be better named. Penne is, in fact, derived from the Celtic word pen, meaning headland or crag.

Many romantic legends are associated with the area round the castle, and this romanticism is reflected in the very walls. One such story tells of Jacques Daure, son of a Montauban inn-keeper, who shone as a student and became private secretary to Talleyrand. In London he met and fell in love with the prince's niece, Princess Dorothée de Courlandes, but she responded to his infatuation with no more than condescending friendship.

In the autumn of 1834 Daure was out on his horse when he discovered Penne. He stayed there a month, wandering in melancholy fashion about the village streets. One evening he celebrated a 'Mass for the Dead' in the church. The following day a loud report echoed across the valley. Daure had killed himself with a revolver on the rocky crag amidst the remains of the château.

Before his death he had made detailed arrangements for his burial, and had asked (and his request was granted) to be buried on the spot where he died. 'Let there be placed upon my heart the graven jewel which my hand was holding at the moment of my death', he wrote. This jewel, a ring in the shape of a coiled serpent, had been a gift to him from the princess.

Pech Grignal
(see map ref R)

8Km
2:15

D15 road
Vaour
Detour *10 mins*
🏠 ✕ ⛲

Ignore the white and red waymarkings of the GR46 leading north to Saint-Antonin-Noble-Val. Beyond the hairpin bend, the GR de Pays turns right (south-east) and goes up to the plateau. Turn east-north-east along the edge of the plateau to Fabret. Carry straight on along an old track through some woods to Fabre de la Grange. The GR turns right, crosses the next bend in the D168 and goes along the road to Belaygue. Cross a stream and go up a track (south-east) to Saint-Pantaléon. Opposite the church take a wide track on the right. Further up, go left along the edge of a meadow to Alic farm. From there, follow the road to the intersection with the D15.

The GR footpath goes to the right along the D15 road for some metres and then, at a wayside cross, turns left towards La Métairie Blanche. Beyond the barn, follow the track (north-east) to La Peyre farm, then the tarmac

Vaour — the name probably meant 'ravine' — owes its existence to the Templars, who established the headquarters of an important command post on a hill at the site.

14Km
3:45

MARNAVES

4Km
1:15

track to the dolmen at Vaour. From there cross the D91 and take a paved track near the picnic area. In another 1.5 kilometres turn right, into a fir plantation, and go down a trail into the Laussière valley. Then turn right and cross the stream, going on to the next intersection. If you carry straight on (south-east) from this intersection you can go direct to Le Pech Agut. The route is shown as a broken line on the map.

The GR follows the road left from this inter-section, up beside a meadow. Go round to the south of Blanquefort, then to the right along a track to Pas de la Clède. Turn right at that point and, in a short distance, right again along a field. The GR goes south, close by Pech Agut, then swings east to a transformer at the intersection of the Marnaves and Peyralade roads. From this junction, go north for 200 metres towards Roussayrolles (see map ref c).

The GR does not go into Roussayrolles. Instead, it goes down to the right along a wide track. At the spring called *Mère de Dieu* (Mother of God) go north-east up a track among some chestnut trees, pass a quarry and go to the right of La Sédarié. Further on, cross the D9 road. Carry straight on (east) to the hamlet of La Beuze. Fork left (north-east) along a wide track. At the next intersection turn right (south-east). The pathway goes down into a little valley, and along by a stream, and takes you into Marnaves.

From Marnaves the GR goes down to the D600 road. Cross the railway track and go across the bridge over the Cérou. Carry on along the D7 road for 200 metres and take a track to the left which is tarmac to begin with and later becomes paved. This goes up (east-south-east) to Latreyne hamlet, from where you take the road heading east. At the crossroads take the right-hand fork to La Védillerie. Before the outskirts, turn right on to the track beside the vineyard which leads to La Védillerie.

LA VÉDILLERIE

From the *gîte d'étape* at La Védillerie, go east along the road for 100 metres and then to the right, down a pathway into the Cérou valley. Go to the right along the D7 road. Just beyond the mill at La Bogne, cross the Cérou by the 'Pont des Anes' and go left along the D91 to the village of Les Cabannes. From there go up and to the right (south-west) towards Les Crozes.

5Km
1:15

Les Crozes

Junction with footpath GR36 which goes south towards Cahuzac-sur-Vère (see page 137).

To continue with the footpath, GR de Pays, follow the white and red waymarkings of the GR36, to the left (eastwards), which will lead you to the outskirts of Cordes.

CORDES
(see map ref D)

To continue the Penne circular tour, follow the GR36 south (page 135). It then continues with the GR de Pays at Coustous.

The GR46 comes from Cahuzac-sur-Vère (see map ref M) to Coustous farm (see page 137).

Coustous
(see map ref E)

From Coustous farm the GR de Pays fords Mouline stream and goes between two fields, climbs the embankment, skirts a meadow and brings you to the road. Walk on along it to the left heading for Larroque, then keep west along a hilltop path. At Poulvrel farm go down to the right and cross the bridge over the Vère. Take the D1 road heading right, and then the next road on the left. Just this side of Saint-Paul farm take the right-hand track towards the dolmen. At a hut, take the right-hand road and drop down towards Lamothe farm. When you reach Laval farm, cut across a bend in the road opposite. Beyond Jouzelles, go left along a pathway. At the next intersection keep going north-west (passing to the west of Pech de Jouzelles), then walk to the right along the La Dugarié road. Just after there, ignore the road which goes right in the direction of Saint-Beauzile. Instead keep heading generally north along a track which becomes a pathway going up to some crossroads.

9Km
2:30

The GR carries straight on and in another 100 metres comes to a fork (see map ref F).

Crossroads
(spot height 357)

Detour 20 mins
LES GRÈZES
⌂ ✕

*This is a well-known horse-
riding centre.
Stay on the road and head
north. The route is indicated
on the map by a dotted line.*

12Km
3:15

At the fork (see map ref f) the GR goes along the left-hand track (north-west) towards Les Cabanes. As you reach the outskirts turn left towards the forest of Grésigne, up to the Pas de Caillaret. From there, go straight down into the forest and come to the Baronde road. Go to the right along this (north-west) as far as some large crossroads called Pas de Pontraute. From there, follow the road heading left and then go up a wide trail and a pathway (north-west) to the hamlet of Haute-Serre.

Take the road down to the right and turn into the first track on the left leading to Font-Blanque. From there, carry on westwards along a cart track. Ignore a track off to the right and walk along by an enclosure. Go left and down into the woods to Fontanelles spring, cross the stream and come back up the other side to Font-Bonne. Then take the D87 road to the right (north-west) as far as a bend (Pas de la Lignée), and there go straight ahead along the road towards Bayès. Follow

Agriculture in the Montmiralais region
Agriculture in the *Land of Vère and Grésigne* is directly affected by the geological characteristics of the soils in the region. Whilst the Triassic and Permian sandstones of the Massif de Grésigne are planted with forests, the limestone plateaux of the Causses are well suited to vinegrowing, whereas the soils in the Vère valley, are more suitable for cereals and fodder crops.

The realignment of the Vère between 1970 and 1978, together with land redistribution and drainage operations, considerably improved the potential for agricultural production in the valley.

Some 75 per cent of the farms in the region are under 25 hectares in size. With operations on such a small scale, it is understandable that the farming population of Castelnau Canton has decreased by 25 per cent in 10 years. Sadly, this statistic goes hand in hand with the other fact to emerge from the *Tour of the Gorges de l'Aveyron*, namely that in the century between the censuses of 1876 and 1975 the region lost practically 60 per cent of its population!

Mixed crop farming is the main system of agriculture in the region, which tends to be oriented around two main divisions: cereals and animals to the west of the Castelnau Canton; vines and cereals in the southern and south-eastern parts of the Canton, which is the northern fringe of the Gaillac winegrowing area, with a reputation for high quality, full-bodied wines.

Highly diversified agriculture along traditional lines, together with wine-growing are the backbone of the local economy, although cattle breeding and forestry make a considerable contribution.

PENNE
⌂ ✕ 🚂 🚃 🚺
(see map ref B)

3Km
0:45

Pech Grignal
(see map ref R)
Over to the right (south-east)
is the junction with the local
footpath, GR de Pays,
leading to Cordes.

6Km
1:30

Cazals
Junction with a minor
footpath, PR, which is
waymarked in yellow and
indicated on the map as a
broken line. This can be
used as an alternative route
along the right bank. It
rejoins the GR footpath at
Brousses hamlet.

4Km
1

Vieil Four
Junction with another minor
footpath, PR, waymarked in
yellow, which can be used
as an alternative route to the
GR. It is shown by the
broken line on the map.

4Km
1:15

this road to the second farm. The road becomes a wide track called *ancienne route de Gaillac* (old Gaillac road). Take this track for 1.5 kilometres dropping down towards Penne.

This is the end of the GR de Pays circular tour starting and finishing at Penne. It is also the junction with the GR46.

The GR46 leaves Penne along the disused railway track of the Montauban to Lexos line, parallel with the main road. Cross the D115 road and go straight ahead along a grass track between the road and the river. The track intersects the road, crosses Amiel hamlet and climbs up on to the Causse via a large winding bend. This brings you to the foot of Pech Grignal.

The GR46 continues towards the north-west and hugs the cliffs which tower above the river Aveyron (Rochers de Biouzac). The wide path heads north-east and brings you to the Pech de Peloffe (362 metres). At the Pech de Peloffe go left (north-west) on to a path which passes the Saint-Antonin shooting range. Drop down through Combe Longue to the dam where there is a footbridge at Cazals.

The GR46 does not cross the footbridge at Cazals, but takes a parallel track opposite and below the D115 road heading north-west. At the fork, this side of the tunnel, go left on to road D115b and then up to the right on a track leading to Brousses. From Brousses hamlet the GR continues along the D115b, and gives you splendid views over the Aveyron valley. Continue to the Vieil Four hamlet.

From Vieil Four the GR leaves the road and goes up a pathway onto the plateau; amongst box trees and junipers is the Petit-Jean estate. From there go down a pathway to the D115 road, cross it and take a cart track between the river and the road, coming to the bridge over the Aveyron. Cross it and enter Saint-Antonin-Noble-Val.

SAINT-ANTONIN-NOBLE-VAL

🏠 ⌂ Ⓧ ⚔ 🚂 🚌 🚩
(see map ref S)

14Km
3:45

The GR46 leaves Saint-Antonin via the D958 road heading west. At the road sign marking the exit from the village, go up a steep pathway to the right. Once on the plateau, pass the ruined chapel of Pech Dax. Then pass the farm until you are level with the shed, and walk along the main drive. As you leave the property, bear right on to a track suitable for vehicles. At an iron crucifix go left along the road (northwest). In another 800 metres take the right-hand grass pathway between low walls. From David farm go downwards heading north and then northeast along a pathway to Gourgue stream. Turn left beside this stream to the spring. In another 50 metres take the right-hand track beneath overhanging trees by a little stream called the Frayssinet, which is dry in summer. In another kilometre go to the right, up a pathway to an intersection marked with a stone cross (spot height 303).

From here, the GR46 turns left. It keeps going straight ahead (northeast), crosses two roads in succession and further on comes to the D926. Go to the right along this road and then, in another 50 metres, go left towards the Hotel Bellevue, then towards a wooden cross from where there is a view over Caylus. At the intersection turn right and go down to Caylus.

CAYLUS

🏠 Ⓧ ⚔ 🚂 🚌 🚩
(see map ref T)

The GR46 leaves Caylus by a steep, grassy path which goes up from the D926 road. Follow the ridge northwards and on a level with Fournet farm go down to the right towards Notre-Dame-de-Livron.

The sanctuary of Notre-Dame-de-Livron is located in a 'cirque' or hollow among rocky cliffs. Such cliffs are typical of limestone areas, and are sometimes said to be 'out of the way' or 'at the ends of the earth'. A caption in the grotto tells the story of the knight of Lagardelle who, with the support of the Virgin Mary, vanquished the dragon which emerged from its lair to devour maidens and youths. There is an annual pilgrimage to the site.

Walk first along the right bank of the stream and then along the left bank. Turn left on to the D19 road. Beyond the bridge go down to the

Caylus

The town stands on a narrow rocky promontory on the side of the Bonnette valley, clearly visible from the shoulder of the causse towering above. The rocky outcrop at its summit is topped with the ruins of a fortified castle which was destroyed in the French Revolution. In the 11th century Caylus depended on the Counts of Toulouse, and this situation continued until 1369, when the supremacy of the King of France was established. For a short intervening period (1362-1369) the town was held for the English by the lieutenant-general of Guyenne on behalf of King Edward III.

At the beginning of the 13th century, Caylus underwent the Albigensian War. It was reconstructed at the end of the same century and the beginning of the next. The church possibly dates from 1370, the houses in the Rue Droite (Maison des Loups) are more recent (15th century). The covered market with its ancient stone measuring standards is a model of vernacular architecture (16th century). The church is built in a massive Gothic style which is none the less fairly typical of the Midi. The nave is well proportioned and contains a lovely wooden statue of Christ by the modern sculptor Zadkine.

Caylus had an eventful history during the Wars of Religion 1586-1587. The town was capital of the bailliage and governed by the Consuls, which gave rise to serious conflicts. It remained Catholic under the Reformation, whereas the neighbouring little town of Saint-Antonin converted to Calvinism. For eight years, after 1583, there was veritable warfare between the two towns, including battles, pillaging, levying of troops, construction of fortifications, hand-to-hand fighting, espionage and murder, against the backdrop of the fields on the causse or the paths criss-crossing the valley. This persisted until 4 November 1591, when the first Consul of Caylus, with a 'good troop of soldiers', retook Lacapelle-Livron and Loze, which had been taken only the previous day by the Calvinists. 11 days later, a truce was signed to cover ploughing and seedtime, and it is still in force .... The castle was rebuilt several times. It existed early in the 12th century, was rebuilt in the 13th and abandoned in the middle of the 16th, when a comfortable Renaissance-style country seat was built on its southern slope.

right, between the stream and the army camp. In Saint-Pierre-Livron, go left along the road. In another 200 metres go on to a pathway past the château de Mondésir. The GR goes up to the plateau and comes to a road near the chapel of Notre-Dame-des-Graces (on the left; built in 1471 on a spur overlooking the Bonnette valley).

The GR takes the road on the right and enters Lacapelle-Livron.

The village was established around a Commanderie of the Templars which was founded in all probability at the end of the 11th century

9Km
2:15

and was one of the most important in the whole of France. In the village you may notice a little market building roofed in stone slabs.

Leave Lacapelle-Livron heading northeast along the D19 road. On a level with a garage, take a road leading left towards Lugan. At that point go to the right (northeast) along a track leading to a high tension line. The path goes under this twice. Then turn to the right and come to an intersection (spot height 314). From there follow the D19 road left and in another 50 metres, at a stone cross, turn right along a track which leads to Loze.

165

Loze

Loze, once a dependency of the Commanderie of Lacapelle-Livron, was totally laid waste in the Hundred Years War. Its massive, fortified church was reconstructed at the end of the 15th century with a wall-belfry which is quite unusual in the architecture of the region. The church is located on a shoulder of the cliff which overlooks the valley of the Bonnette and the Cirque de Saint Géry.

Before visiting the village itself, which is partly isolated from its surroundings by the land requisitioned for Caylus army base, go to the cirque, or at least as far as a rock-face, at the foot of which some interesting fossils may be found, and take a look at a wash house some tens of metres away. With its spring and the lovely lines of its construction, this is a classic of its type in the region.

The river Bonnette is first class for angling, and a great favourite with trout fishermen. Studded with magnificent mills which are now disused, the river forms a natural boundary between the provinces of Quercy and Rouergue.

LOZE

⌂

(see map reference U)
Junction with the 'GR de Pays' (local footpath) waymarked in yellow and red, from Monteils.

Detour *20 mins*
Saint-Projet

Footpath GR46 leaves Loze by the west and crosses the D19 road. Take the first road on the right beyond the cemetery (northwest). In another 600 metres continue along a grass track to the right. At the next intersection go left on to a track with low walls. In another 400 metres, near the place called Borie-Sèque, go right (due north) and come to the D33b road.

Turn right on to the D33b to visit the village and château of Saint-Projet.

The GR46 crosses the D33b and continues (northeast) along a grassy track. Farther on this crosses the D33. Go straight ahead along a track lined with elms and oaks. In another 2 kilometres, at the bottom of a slope and before reaching the D19, turn left (northwest). Walk along the fields beside the overgrown path. Go by Caussat hamlet, cross a cement bridge and continue via Bournaguet to the D53 road. This brings you to the junction with the GR36 coming from Cahors in the northwest.

The Tour of the Gorges de l'Aveyron takes the D53 to the right (northeast) to Beauregard (see map ref V).

BEAUREGARD

✗ ⚓ ▭

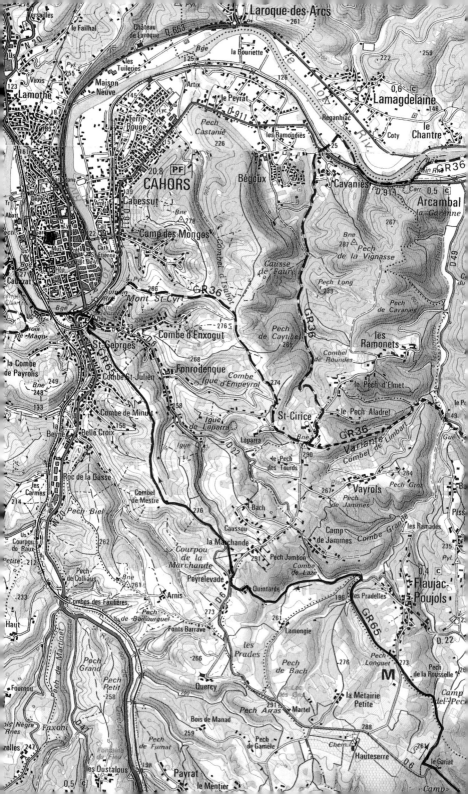

WALK 4

CAHORS

17Km
4:15

The walk begins on the outskirts of Cahors. The GR65 does not enter the town, so from the centre of Cahors you need to cross the River Lot by the Louis-Philippe bridge. (Once over the bridge you will notice the white-and-red striped waymarkings for the GR36 which goes from Cahors to Albi.)

To join the GR65 turn right and walk through the passage under the railway track. At Saint-Georges turn right and take the tarmac path which passes a sunken water tower. The path gradually rises above the Lot Valley and becomes a cart track which goes straight ahead along the ridge. When the track comes to a road, go straight over, thereby cutting off a bend in the road, and rejoin it at a cross.

Turn right a few metres further on. At the fork take the left-hand road which joins the D6.

Turn left for a short distance, then take the track on your left to La Quintarde. Pass the hamlet and follow the track bearing left. After a kilometre you pass some buildings on your right. The track crosses the D22 on the outskirts of the village of Flaujac-Poujols. The track goes along a little valley, crosses a road and enters another little valley Pech-Longuet. The GR65 goes through the valley and up to the plateau. When the path comes to a fork, take the right-hand path and 500 metres further on turn left. The track at this point is quite big, but as it nears Gariat it becomes hardly visible. At Gariat turn left on to the D6 for a short distance and then join the D49 for 400 metres. The GR65 turns right, crosses the Tréboulou stream, and follows a track which turns left and crosses the Cieurac stream. A little further on take a path to the right, pass two mills and walk alongside the stream. The path joins the road that leads up towards Pech hamlet. Go down the road towards the bridge that crosses Cieurac stream, but do not cross

it. Instead, go right along the road to the wash house at Outriols spring.

The GR65 climbs upwards, passing walls made from amazingly large blocks of stone. It crosses the D10, and another road and keeps straight on, taking you to Mas de Vers.

Cahors

In this capital of the province of Quercy, many relics have survived to confirm that this city regularly acted as host to pilgrims heading for Santiago de Compostella.

First, the many-domed Romanesque Cathedral of Saint-Etienne (St Stephen) which was consecrated on 10 September 1119 by Pope Calixtus II and was built on the site of an earlier sanctuary built under freedoms granted by king Dagobert.

In the cloister, a carving on a rectangular stone shows a dispute between two pilgrims, one of whom is recognisable by his shell.

There were several hospitals, one of which was called the Hôpital Saint-Jacques. It was close to the present-day Place Galdemar. Then in 1683 it was transferred to the place known as the Croix des Capucins.

In the 16th century a chapel dedicated to the apostle of Spain became known as Saint-Jacques des Pénitents as soon as it became the seat of a brotherhood of blue penitents. A very interesting altar-piece was kept there.

In the early centuries AD the exit from the town and across the Lot used to be, as today, opposite the Quartier Saint-Georges. Since the 14th century there has also been an exit via the famous Pont Valentré. In those days the pilgrims used to climb a fairly steep path up to the Croix de Magne and from there, with a final backwards glance over the ancient capital of the Cadurces, would resume their journey guided always by the Milky Way.

Cahors, the *Divona Cadurcorum* of antiquity — the sacred spring of the Cadurces — has been the capital of Quercy for two thousand years. Its urban setting is unique. The left bank of the Lot forms a semi-circle of jointed, yellow limestone rock-faces, with steep, rocky, brush-covered slopes. Here and there, houses nestle in the shade of cypress trees which stand out against the sky. Inevitably we are reminded of those charming little landscapes by Giotto. The town suffered many occupations and wars, but throughout the Middle Ages was both a university town and a centre for merchants and money-changers. Cahors is now the préfecture for the département of the lot and a cathedral city. Even though it has lost some of its medieval splendour, its administrative and commerial role makes it a decidedly busy city. It is a centre for trade in, among other things, foie gras, truffles, local ham, goat cheeses, walnut liqueurs, juniper liqueur, plum brandy, prunes, Cahors wines — rosé and white wines produced in the region — and also performed candles, some made to float and others simply but elegantly decorated. Since 1950 buildings have been springing up virtually everywhere. At the same time tourism in Cahors has been developing. Visitors who discover the bustle of the Boulevard Gambetta make the most of it and devote some time to admiring the architectural riches of Cahors.

Mas de Vers
(or Mas d'Abert)
Named after a plateau in the area. Excavations have uncovered Gallo-Roman sarcophagi close to the Roman road. This is notable for its almost straight course. At one time it was a merchant route connecting Cahors to Caylus. Pilgrims avoided the road because it was badly maintained, isolated, and also because it was difficult to find lodgings, provisions and places of worship on the way.

9Km
2:15

BACH
✕ ♆ ⚓
The village is named after a German family which moved here in the 18th century, and many local families still bear this surname. Phosphate used to be quarried here.

1Km
0:15

Mas de Dégot
Junction with GR36 from Concots and Bouziès.

4Km
1

La Plane
Detour *15 mins*
VARAIRE

The line of the GR65 is very obvious all along the way since it follows an ancient footpath for about 15 kilometres. It crosses the D26, the D55, Valses stream, and the D42 road (Escamp-Vaylats). The GR65 leaves the Roman road soon after crossing the D42 and takes a grassy path on the left to the village of Bach.

The GR65 leaves the D19 road outside the village, ignores a road on the left and takes a track which passes the Mas de Gaston and leads to the Mas de Dégot.

From this point the GR65 and GR36-46 follow the same route to La Plane. Shortly after passing the Mas Dégot, the GR65 intersects a road (spot height 301). Here there is a farm on the right which is not named on the map. At this point there is nothing to indicate that the GR36-46 from Concots and Bouziès joins the GR65.

The GR65 continues along a tarmac road which comes out at one of the entrance gates to the Couanac chase. Turn right here and walk along the boundary. The path crosses a little valley where there are many stone slabs. Further on the path is somewhat overgrown with brushwood. At a fork take the right-hand track and carry straight along a paved track. The path crosses the D52 road and enters the hamlet of La Plane.

Go right and follow the waymarking for the GR36-46. The GR36-46 goes towards Albi at this point.

⌂ ✕ ⚓ 🚋

The southern boundary of the district was formed by a very old track called the 'Cami Gasco'. In 1561 there were two inns where travellers could put up. As early as the 13th century a hospital and church, known as Saint-Jacques-de-Peyronèse, were receiving pilgrims. There is a cross on a little dry-stone wall marking the site, which the villagers call the Croix de Pétronille.

7Km
1:45

The GR65 passes through the hamlet towards Pech Coiniere. At the intersection with a road turn left and a few metres further on left again on to a track. Follow it for a few metres and turn left. At a small place called Bousigue the GR turns abruptly right. A little further on where the path meets a road, follow it to the right, keep going until you come to another road. Cross this road and in another kilometre the path enters the woods. It leads downwards and eventually becomes a track between low walls and comes to a hollow. Continue along the path and go through two gates (remember to close them). GR65 goes up through the woods and comes to a road. Take the left-hand fork. Stay on the road for 250 metres till you come to the wayside cross (spot height 292). Ignoring the track to the left the path carries on and passes a farm at Ferrières-Bas where you can buy goat's cheese. A little further on ignore the tarmac road off to the left, and another off to the right. Follow the path through the woods. It comes out on to a paved track which then becomes tarmac. Carry straight on, passing a stone cross, until the track meets the D19 road on the outskirts of Limogne-en-Quercy.

LIMOGNE-EN-QUERCY

🏨 ⌂ ⛺ ✕ ⚓ 🚋

Was a junction for all travellers and pilgrims crossing the Causse, because at that time the

The GR65 does not go into the town, and 500 metres after crossing the D19 it turns right on to the D24 for about 50 metres. It then goes towards Mas de Bassoul. In a while you turn right out of a side street and carry straight on. The track meets the D911 and goes up

winding course of the Lot could not be crossed by road.

between low walls. It passes a track on the right, goes through some trees, down towards a cultivated area, and rises again, bearing right.

Just after you pass a farm wall turn left. Take the next track to the left. This brings you to the Mas de Palat. Turn right on to the D143 and 400 metres further on turn left on to a well-made track. When it joins the road turn right and go straight ahead for 150 metres to the wayside cross. At the Mas de Dalat the path rises to the Mas de la Teule where there are some derelict houses. Turn left and, following the waymarkings carefully, enter the wood. The path comes out alongside a wood, go right and emerge at a bend on the D19. Stay on the local road to the Mas de Bories. Turn left on to a track and at the next intersection turn right. Ignore the next track on the left, and the one on the right, and in another 800 metres turn left on to a cart track. Go straight ahead, cross the D79 and enter Mas del Pech.

8Km
2

Mas del Pech

Take the D79 road to the right as far as Saint-Jean. Some 2 kilometres to the south-east of Saint-Jean is the swallow hole known as Gouffre de l'Oule.

Detour *15 mins*
SAINT-JEAN-DE-LAUR

The GR leaves the hamlet along a track which goes through crops and among trees to the Mas de Dugarel where there are some derelict houses with stone slab roofs. Carry on along the path to a fork and take the pebbly track on the left. Further on it goes through a gate (close it carefully) and turns right. Go up the track and, before reaching the top of Pech Niol, turn left. About 400 metres along the road you will be close to the Mas de Couderc, opposite and below to the right. Follow the waymarkings carefully as the GR goes through a wood of junipers, oaks and box trees. The path descends giving you a view of the château at Gaillac. Go straight along the road when the GR joins it to the outskirts of Gaillac.

6Km
1:30

Gaillac

Take the GR footpath through Gaillac, follow the road to the right, cross the Lot by the suspension bridge and turn left. Go straight along the road, passing to the right of a

4Km
1

CAJARC

🏠 ⌂ ⛺ 🍴 🚂 🚌 🛈

*Situated at the foot of a
group of limestone cliffs;
popular stopping place for
the pilgrims to Santiago de
Compostela. Chapel of La
Madeleine, called locally 'la
Capelette de Cajarc', dates
from 12th century.
25-metres high waterfall
nearby called La Caoûgne.
Among cliffs to the north is
Roc de Conte and on hillside
the Château des Anglais. At
Saut de la Mounine is a view
over the valley and the the
Lot. Footpath passes
chancel of 12th-century
leper hospital chapel.*

6Km
1:30

Le Verdier

*The alternative route from
Cajarc meets the GR65 at
the crossroads (spot height
316).*

4Km
1

wayside cross. Go right along the D662 for
250 metres. Walk down on to a pathway which
goes through a kitchen garden, turn left and
walk alongside the railway. Opposite a tunnel
under the railway track, the GR enters a street
and turns left on to the D662 and the outskirts
of Cajarc.

Alternative route to La Verdier (1hr 30mins).
This is shown as a dotted line on the map and
is waymarked with two horizontal and two
vertical parallel stripes. Leave Cajarc on the
D19 heading right. Go up a limestone track
heading due north. Go through a gate and a
little further on, where the track turns right, go
to the left. The track goes between low stone
walls and comes to the D19. Turn right and 50
metres further on, turn left. The road goes right
(north-east) and then north and becomes a
tarmac track which takes you into Le Verdier.

The GR65 leaves Cajarc on the D662 and
takes a path on the right just before the quarry.
A little further on turn left on to a grass path
which climbs up, passes a vast cavern and
goes along the cliff. When the path joins a
tarmac track turn left along it for 100 metres.

Turn left, cross a road and follow the path
between low stone walls. A little further on at
the wayside cross go over the road and follow
the path bearing right (north). The GR passes
some buildings on the right and takes a track
which rises gently and crosses a road. On the
left you will see a restored mill and a TV mast.
The GR follows a hilltop track, turns right and
goes down to another road. It crosses a
narrow road where there is a crucifix and takes
a track which becomes tarmac. At the crossroads (spot height 316) the footpath turns left
into Le Verdier.

The GR65 turns left at the crossroads on to a
tarmac track to Le Pigeonnier. The path
gradually rises, crosses another track, passes
Martigne farm and joins a path which goes
alongside a stone wall. The footpath bears
slightly to the right and along a track which
crosses the D82. It goes up to a crossroads
where there is the oldest stone cross in the

GRÉALOU

⌂ ✗ 🛤 🚃

The Romanesque church of Notre Dame de l'Assomption has beautiful 17th-century Descent from the Cross and 1664 stone font with carvings. Many dolmens in the surrounding area.

9Km
2:15

BÉDUER

⌂ ▲ ♟ 🛤

Fortress once held sway over all territory between the Lot and the Célé, rivalling Figeac abbey.

4Km
1

region and an imposing dolmen. The GR65 goes right (north) on to a track which goes along a ridge. It comes out alongside a cemetery wall and takes you into Gréalou.

The GR65 leaves the village, taking a street on the left, then on the right, passing to the right of the reservoir. The footpath crosses the D19, goes left along the road and takes a winding path on the left. It joins a road, turns right for 100 metres, then goes left on to a cart track. The track gets narrower as it rises among the trees. It comes out on the D38 and turns left for 250 metres. It turns right on to a path which passes Pech Favard and becomes a sunken lane. At the intersection turn left and pass Combe-Salgues farm. At the Mas de Surgues the GR turns right, then left a little further on at the road, and then right. The footpath takes a track which rises, turns left, continues to rise and passes between low walls. At a bend, near Pech Rougié, the GR joins a road, turns right on to the D19 and takes you into Béduer.

Alternative route To avoid Béduer and rejoin the GR65, turn right (north-east) to Pech Rougié. The route is shown on the map as a dotted line.

Near the cemetery is the waymarking for the GR651 which runs along the valley of the Célé as far as its confluence with the Lot, near Bouziès, where it joins the GR36. It is then possible to follow the GR36 to Cahors, where it meets the GR65 again, or to Saint-Cirq-Lapopie, Varaire and Villefranche-de-Rouergue, then through the Aveyron gorges to Cordes, the GR36-46 Cahors-Albi.

From Béduer church the GR65 takes the road on the left to Mas de Capus, where there is a cross, and keeps straight on passing the Mas de la Croix. The path goes on passing the intersection with the Lascamp road (spot height 327).

At this point, to reach the tented gîte d'étape at La Vaysse turn right (see dotted line on map).

The path continues and joins the D21 road into Faycelles.

FAYCELLES
�֍ ⛟

6Km
1:30

The GR65 turns left near a stone cross and continues along a road which crosses the D622. A little further on at the crossroads where there is a crucifix take the right-hand road which goes through the hamlet of Ferrières. Just past the Trévepau the path takes a short-cut on the left and rejoins the road. The footpath goes along a ridge and then along a sunken lane passing to the left at Cassagnole hamlet and to the right of Buffan. The track continues straight ahead, and at the junction of a road turns right for 500 metres to Malaret. Stay on the tarmac road for a kilometre when the path joins the D922 at Capelo where there is a stone cross. Turn left to Aiguille du Cingle.

Aiguille du Cingle
One of four 13th-century obelisks believed to mark boundaries of the Benedictine abbey founded in 755 by Pépin the Short.

Junction of GR65 and GR6.

2.5Km
0:45

The GR65 takes a road along a limestone plateau. It leads you to a path which goes down a Cingle hill (from the Latin cingula meaning belt or enclosure). It enters a farm yard, turns right and then left, and a little further on goes under a railway bridge. The GR65 goes along a street, turns right by the electricity office and takes the second turning on the right into Figeac via the Avenue Jean-Jaurès.

FIGEAC
⌂ ⌂ ⛺ ✗ ⅄ ⚒ ⛟
⛟ ℹ
Described as one of the most intriguing towns in France.
Old town with twisting streets and fine range of medieval buildings. The solheilho, (roofed, open-sided loft) and corbelled turret are typical

From the Tourist Information Office go towards the church of Saint-Thomas and take the road to the camping site at Les Carmes. Walk along by Planioles stream for 4 kilometres following the road which is not used much. Pass the hamlet of La Curie, which used to belong to the Templars. The stream now flows between volcanic rocks and sandstone. The road comes to a meadow which you cross. On the left, you will see large spoil tips outside some old zinc mines. They sometimes turn up ore mineralizations of blende and galena.

Figeac – A brief history

Historical documents tell us that in 838 Pépin of Aquitaine founded an establishment for the monks of Conques, who set up in the little 'cella' of Saint-Martin of Lunan.

This place of worship may have formed the original nucleus for the population before being destroyed when the river Lot flooded. Was the settlement transferredto the hill above the town of Figeac? This is certainly possible, since the first of the abbots were buried there, and traces of Gallo-Roman buildings were discovered near the church of Notre Dame du Puy.

A manuscript of 972 mentions the monastery on the edge of the river Célé. At that time, therefore, the abbey had already been built on the spot occupied today by the abbey church of Saint-Sauveur and the monks from Conques were already in occupation. At about this period the sanctuary may have been enriched with the relics of Saint Vivien and Saint Marcel, which some monks are reputed to have stolen from Saintes. Part of the church was then dedicated to bishop Saint Vivian. About the middle of the 11th century a dispute arose between the abbeys of Conques and Figeac, and a long-lasting rivalry split the founding abbey from its former offshoot. The latter's independence was not finally recognised until 1096 by decision of the Council of Nîmes.

In 1074, the monks of Figeac had elected as their abbot Hugues-de-Cluny, whose protection was to make it possible to construct a substantial abbey church. The construction of the building which we admire today began around 1130-1150 but was suddenly interrupted. Work began again in the 13th century. The buildings suffered badly during the Hundred Years War and the Wars of Religion. This fine example of a church said to be of the pilgrimage type is similar in concept to the basilicas of Conques and of Saint Sernin in Toulouse. The chapter house, also known as Notre-Dame de Pitié (Our Lady of Mercy) is remarkable for a series of ornate 17th-century wooden panels. Among the interesting capitals (some of which can be seen in the south aisle) are some carved with shells, in commemoration of the pilgrims passing by on their way to Santiago de Compostella.

The church of Notre Dame du Puy, above the town, used to be called Notre Dame la Fleurie. This successor to a Carlovingian sanctuary was built from the 12th century onwards, with extensive alterations in the 13th and 14th centuries. It was ravaged in the Hundred Years War and by the Portestants. There is a large altar-piece with paintings on the theme of the glorification of the Virgin Mary. This work by Jean Lofficial dates from 1683. One of its chapels was the seat of a brotherhood of St James and houses a fine statue of the apostle. The statue is now in the museum at Rocamadour.

Figeac was important as a stopping-place for pilgrims, and there were several hospitals sheltering travellers and the poor. They included the Hôpital du Griffoul and the Hôpital Saint Eutrope, but of especial significance were the Hôpital Saint Namphaise opposite the abbey church Saint Sauveur, which gave refuge to passing merchants and pilgrims, and the Hôpital d'Augou, founded before 1260, which survives today under the name of the Hôpital Saint Jacques.

Interesting features of the town include the Hôtel de la Monnaie, an elegant 13th-century Gothic building which houses a museum. The Maison des Templiers in the Place Champollion reminds us that this military order had a commandery here. Traces of the veneration of St. James are also to be found in a painting in the church of St Thomas, not far from the hospital, and a street flanked with remains of fortifications known as Rue Saint-Jacques.

Recent excavations have uncovered the remains of walls dating from Gallo-Roman times. But the city did not become very important until the 11th and 12th centuries. Because it is between Conques and Moissac, on the route to Santiago de Compostela, many pilgrims stopped off on their way through. In the 14th century, government by the abbot — who was the lord of the manor of Figeac — passed into the hands of the elected consuls, and the city became subject to the king. The town then had its own Mint.

During the Hundred Years War, Figeac resisted English domination and was not taken by force until 1372. The occupation lasted a year. During the Wars of Religion, having adopted the Protestant faith in 1576, Figeac was taken by the armies of Louis XIII. Its citadel and its walls were levelled (1622). In the 17th and 18th centuries much work was carried out which altered the appearance of the town. Gates were removed and moats filled in; a wharf and a chestnut market were constructed.

Today this old town with the twisting streets has one of the finest ranges of medieval buildings to be found in France. The 'solheilho', the roofed, open-sided loft which gave fresh air on a warm summer's evening, and the corbelled turret rising generally above the roof tops, are typical features of Quercy architecture which can be seen in many streets of old Figeac. Commercially the present day city is very bustling, with mechanical engineering, trade exhibitions and a highly regarded centre for business transactions.

A window in Figeac

10Km
2:30

features of Quercy architecture. Places of particular interest: Saint-Sauveur church, 11th and 14th centuries; Hotel de la Monnaie (Mint), 13th century; Champollion Museum, including a replica of the Rosetta Stone; church of Notre-Dame-du-Puy, 11th and 14th centuries; Aiguilles du Cingle (neighbouring hills).

At the end of the meadow, cross the little bridge over the stream and go up a fairly steep path into sight of Château Favard (16th and 17th centuries). Go to the right of the château along a tarmac path.

Past two bends you come to the D15 road, go to the right for 200 metres, turn left and carry along a tarmac road. A little further on, beyond a thicket, go to the right on to a path. This comes to a road which you take heading right, then to the D15 where you head north to Cardaillac.

CARDAILLAC

🏠 🍴 ⚓ 🚌

*Birthplace of a famous
Quercy family, the
Cardaillacs. Remains of a
fortress: two square towers
(11th and 12th centuries)
and one round tower (15th
century). Many medieval
houses. A pathway goes
around the old fortress, from
where you can overlook the
Drauzou valley.*

4Km
1

Go through the village and left along the
fortress footpath. Go down to Navarre mill and
cross the Drauzou. Then go left up a steep
pathway through a chestnut grove and among
heather to a pond which you can bathe in
during the summer. Walk round to the right of
it. At the edge of the pond, take a path to the
right, then turn left at the next intersection. You
will pass the hamlet of Arlès and then come to
Saint-Bressou.

Saint-Bressou

5Km
1:15

At the intersection of the D92 and D15 roads
where there is a wayside cross, take the D92
for 30 metres and then turn west on to a track
joining up with a road. Go right (north) along
this road as far as Le Poteau farm. At that point
turn right (north) down a pathway through a
chestnut grove, coming to a road which you
follow to the D15. Go left (west) along the D15
to Lacapelle-Marival.

LACAPELLE-MARIVAL

🏠 ⌂ ⛺ 🍴 🍷 ⚓ 🚌
🛈

*13th-century castle;
15th-century church in the
town centre, beyond the
gate within the old walls;
15th-century market building
on massive stone columns.*

4Km
1

Cross the village and leave by the N140 Le
Bourg road. Before reaching an electricity
transformer, go to the right along the D11
road. In another kilometre, at the crossroad
carry on in the same direction to the N681, turn
on to it heading right and go into Rudelle.

Rudelle

*Fortified church with a
rampart walk (13th century).*

4Km
1

Go through the village along a road running
parallel with the N681. Then take the N681
road for 100 metres. Just before the cemetery
where there is a wayside cross, go to the right
up a gently rising track to the plateau and turn
left (north) when you come to the road. Beyond
Peyrou farm and this side of the D15 road, turn
sharp left (west) along a tree-lined track. This
track turns northwards and to the left of the
buildings at Le Bouysset. You skirt the D15
road at the wayside cross and carry on along
a little road to the water tower. Beyond this
tower turn left, along a little path which brings
you to the D38 road, close to Rueyres.

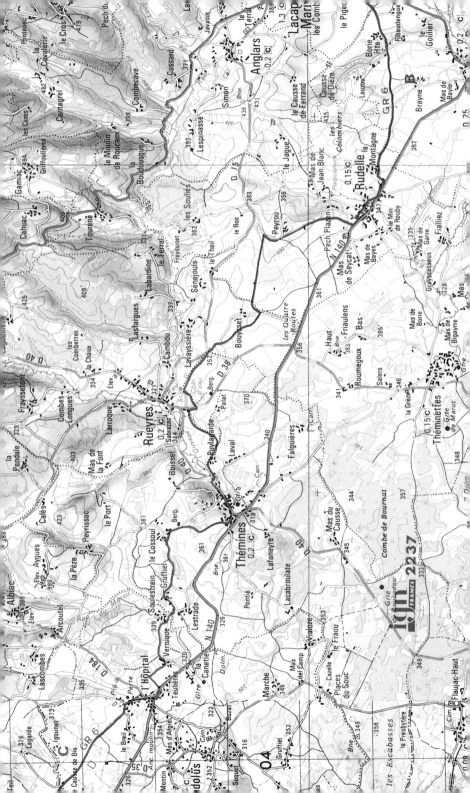

Rueyres

2Km
0:30

THEMINES
🏠 🍴 🍷 ⚓

The stream disappears in the village, and is believed to re-emerge at the springs at Cabouy, 20 kilometres away, which feed the River Ouysse on a level with Cabouy mill near Rocamadour.

4Km
1

L'Hôpital de Beaulieu
Hospice for pilgrims, formerly belonging to the Knights of the Order of St John of Jerusalem (13th century).

7Km
1:45

GRAMAT
🏠 ⛺ 🍴 ⚓ 🚌 🚆 🛈

At the centre of the Causse de Gramat, which is named after it. One of the cities of Haut-Quercy most severely affected by Hundred Years War and Wars of Religion. Only clock tower and market buildings still give any idea of its vanished splendour. Nowadays, a relatively important centre for trade fairs and sheep and horse markets.

5Km
1:15

The GR footpath crosses the D38, avoiding the village, and goes straight ahead along a track passing to the left of the barns at Mas de Sol. Cross Ouysse stream, and go to the left along the road into Themines.

Cross the village, and beyond the second café go to the top of the village. Take the track between two low walls which leads to the hamlet of Cossoul. On reaching the outskirts go left (west) along a grass path which becomes a road. You pass the Gruffiel and Lestrade farms in turn, bearing to their right. Cross a stream and go up towards the Soulestrain and Vernique farms. A pathway brings you to the N681 road. Turn right onto the road which takes you to the village square at L'Hôpital de Beaulieu.

From the square, take the Bio road. At the top of the village, at the crossroads take the left-hand road which goes north-west across the plateau. In another 1500 metres, cross the access road to Lagarde farm on the right; 500 metres further on the road turns north. Ignore the turning and carry straight on along a tree-lined track until you come to the N681 road. Follow this to the left for 100 metres, then turn right, on to a little road which goes along by the Alzou stream. Cross the stream and go into Gramat.

The GR footpath leaves the town by the Rue Saint-Roch and then the Rue du Calvaire, going alongside the cemetery wall to cross-roads where it turns left and crosses Alzou stream. Follow a bend in the road and then walk alongside the railway for a few metres. Turn left under the railway bridge on to a grass path. This brings you to a little road which you follow to the right. In another 200 metres go left along a pathway flanked by trees which becomes a sunken lane with 'clédos' (hurdles). Please be sure to close them again behind you. Keep going north-west along the road to Baillot farm. From there, take a path which continues north-west to Lauzou hamlet. Go through Lauzou and take a track between low walls, which brings you to a car park. Turn right, go down a pathway and across the

Alzou stream. If you are on horseback, carry straight on up a pathway on to the Causse, as it is not possible for horses to cross at the Moulin du Saut.

Pont du Moulin du Saut

Between Moulin du Saut and Boulégou mill is the Grotte de la Roque Fumade on the opposite bank, and the derelict mills of Tournefeuille, Mouline and Sirogne. In 19th century there were twelve mills operating on the Alzou, which rises at Marinhac-Lentour. Between the mills at Tournefeuille and Sirogne, are remains of ovens used during the Second World War for manufacturing charcoal. Very tall willows (over thirty metres high) date from that time.

This section of GR footpath, between the Moulin du Saut and Rocamadour, is impassable in wet weather. Footpath GR6 crosses the bridge over the Alzou and turns left along the stream. Cross the Moulin du Saut by the inside staircase, following the safety barrier up the hillside, coming down again to the bottom of the Alzou gorge. From this point the GR6 follows the course downstream for about 3 kilometres, crossing the stream here and there but never straying far from it, as far as Boulégou mill. If you are coming on horseback from Rocamadour, leave the GR at the Tournefeuille mill. A pathway goes left up to the Causse.

Detour *30 mins*
BLANAT-LE-SOUCI
⌂

7Km
2

Detour see left. Carry on up the pathway opposite the bridge, on to the Causse. At the railway line turn left, follow it to a tunnel and turn to the right under the track. This brings you to the N140 road on to which you turn right. In another 200 metres turn left (north) on to a pathway (on the right notice the swallow-hole called Saut de la Pucelle). You come to the gîte d'étape at Le Souci.

Beyond Boulégou mill the path becomes a stony track, leaves the wood but stays close to the course of the Alzou until nearly at the camping site. Ignore a road on the left which crosses the Alzou towards the village of Couzou. Walkers who wish to visit Rocamadour and L'Hospitalet should go on a few metres more along the road to the right and follow the waymarks for the GR46, which intercepts the GR6 at this point.

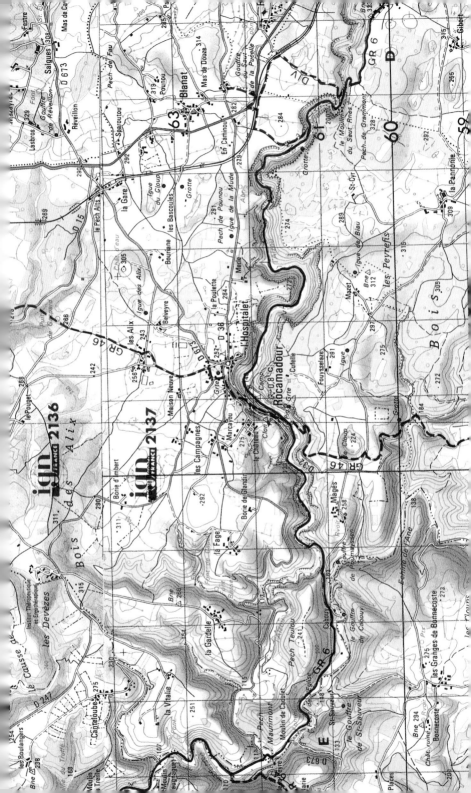

ROCAMADOUR

🏠 ⚑ ✕ ⚒ 🚌 🚃 ℹ

Many places of interest here: lovely views over area from L'Hospitalet or Couzou road; remains of a château, a hospital and the palace of the bishops of Tulle; chapel of the Black Madonna sought by pilgrims; old city (13th to 15th centuries) and its narrow streets; church; house of Marot; Grotte des Merveilles. In surrounding area: springs at Cabouy and Saint-Sauveur (flowing swallow-holes), Saut de la Pucelle swallow-hole, gorges of the Alzou and the Ouysse.

6.5Km
1:45

MOULIN DE CAOULET
⚑

0.5Km
0:15

Pont de la Peyre
The mill at Caugnaguet is in working order and listed as a building of historical interest.

7Km
2

LES BERTOUX
🏠 ✕

Detour 15 mins
LACAVE
🏠 ⚑ ✕ ⚒
Visit the caverns which are a 'synthesis of the caverns of France' (Norbet Casteret).

To get back to the GR6 go down to the Alzou along the waymarkings for the GR46 and take the road to the left which goes towards the camping sites and downstream beside the Alzou to a bridge. The GR46 goes off to the left and crosses the Alzou. It goes to Labastide-Murat and the Lot valley.

The GR6 leaves Rocamadour along the hill road between the valleys of the Alzou and the Ouysse. Follow this road for about 3 kilometres. Ignore a track up to the right to Pech-de-Teulou and a road to the left leading to Magès hamlet. A little further on, at a fork, go to the right along a path (the road goes down towards the Cabouy swallow-hole). The path now overlooks the valley of the Ouysse. It brings you to Moulin de Caoulet.

Walk below the porch of Caoulet mill and, a little further on, cross the Alzou by a small bridge before it joins the Ouysse. Ignore the D673 road on the right and carry straight on along the road to Pont de la Peyre.

On crossing the bridge you find the waymarks for the GR64 which goes to Gourdon, Groléjac, Domme, the valley of the Dordogne and Les Eyzies in the Vézère valley, where it rejoins the GR6.

The GR6 continues straight ahead along a paved track beside the Ouysse to the mill at Caugnaguet. You then come to the Treille mill, on the opposite bank, and then the Truffé spring. You then notice, on the other bank, the hamlets of Bourgnou and Verdoire before coming to Bertoux.

When the GR reaches Les Bertoux, take the road to the right up into the village. Once in Les Bertoux, go down to the Ouysse bridge and cross over. Go to the right and up a winding road to the hamlet of Les Boules. On the outskirts go right, along a track up to the entrance to the Château de Belcastel, overlooking the confluence of the Dordogne and the Ouysse. Go left along the D43 road. In

4Km
1

PINSAC

On left bank of the Dordogne
on cliff above river, you can
see the Château de la
Treyne (16th and 18th
centuries).

6Km
1:30

SOUILLAC

Stands on the right bank of
the Dordogne. Name comes
from old word 'souilh' which
means muddy and
overgrown place; was a
favourite haunt of wild boar.
A boar's head now features
in the town's coat-of-arms.
15th-century abbey which
during the Hundred Years
War was at its height. Town
taken by English in 1351 and
1356 and after rising from its
ruins was again destroyed

another 500 metres turn right and after a little while turn left down a track to the village of Meyraguet. Do not go into the village, but instead go left along a road which joins up with the D43, which you then follow to Port de Pinsac. There go to the right, towards the camping site. This side of the camping site go left along a country path past the cemetery at Pinsac.

From the church square, leave the D96 behind you on the right. At the first crossroads turn right (north) into a street. Cross a path and in another 250 metres turn left. Go through an oak wood, the path continues along the hillside and bears right towards a little valley. Then turn at a sharp angle to the left at the hut and a little futher on, turn right and up to another little hollow (north-west) on a country path through an area re-afforested by the French forestry authority.

Pass to the left of the Combe Lombard and a little further on, come to a track which you take left towards an electricity transformer. Then take the track to Biorouge which, here, is parallel to the Dordogne as far as the Port de Souillac, where the GR turns to the left, intersecting the N20 road, then a minor road, and then follows the Dordogne downstream. Before the municipal camping site take a road on the right going to the centre of Souillac.

The GR6 leaves the département of the Lot and enters the département of the Dordogne. Leave the town by going to the abbey church and taking Rue Louqsor, Avenue Martin-Malvy and Boulevard Beausoleil (from where you have a view over the valley) then left down Avenue de Verdun to the N703 road where you turn right. In another 450 metres turn right, into the Chemin des Marjaudes. This tarmac track takes the GR to the footbridge across the Biard stream, then the railway viaduct for the Paris-Toulouse line above the hamlet. Keep going in the same direction. The path passes to the left of some bare rocks, the surface becomes stony, and brings you to a small barn opposite a small plantation of pines.

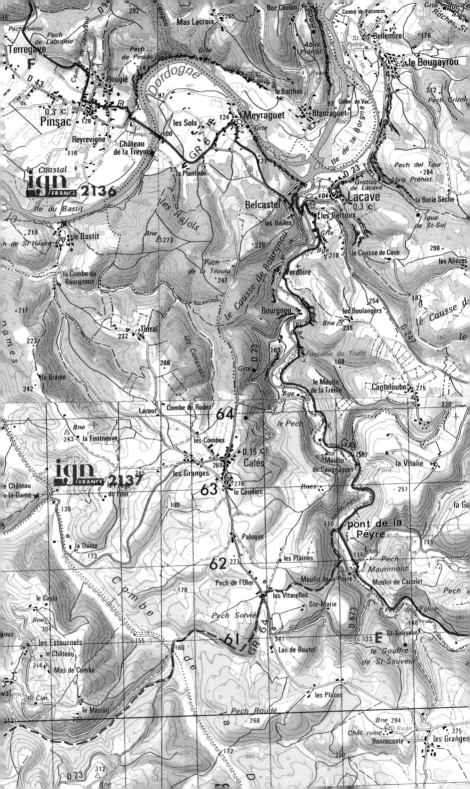

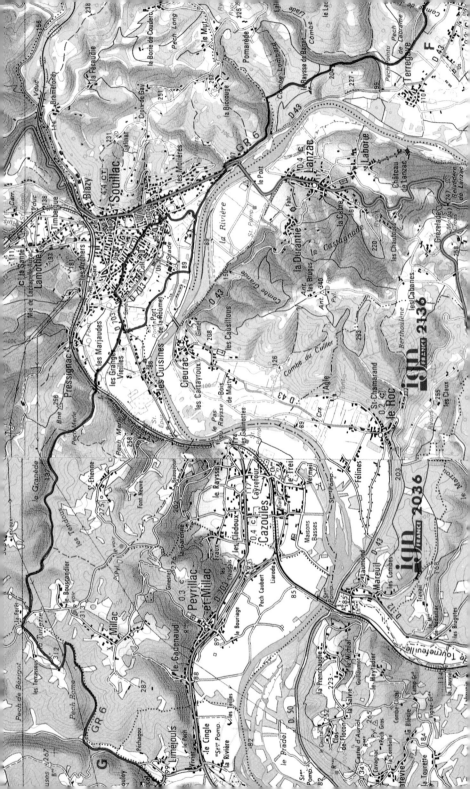

during the Wars of Religion when abbey was sacked. Once powerful and prosperous town declined during the 18th century. Nowadays, an important tourist centre.

Continue heading west. The climb becomes noticeable. You come to a clearing in the woods from which there is a vantage point over the Dordogne valley. The slope becomes gentler and then steepens again. The ground becomes grassy and the going slippery in places, as you pass through a wood of oaks and hornbeams. At a fork, keep straight on. The path keeps climbing before coming out at la Forêt on to the minor road from Bouscandier to Castang. Turn right and follow the road for 250 metres. On the left take a dirt path which heads south-west and passes to the left of Terrassous farm. The GR climbs on to the Causse and reaches the highest point on the route (312 metres). From here you will have a lovely view towards the south-west with the Dordogne at the end of the valley and the slopes of its left bank towards the Château de Fénelon. To the west, the outlines of the Périgordian hills stretch away into the far distance. Carry on to the Pech-Rome farm which is just below, and go around to the left of it.

13Km
3:45

Opposite the little valley, or hollow, go down to the left along an old track flanked with dry stones. In another 400 metres, at a fork, turn right and follow the valley bottom (the 'thalweg') which is overgrown in places. The path widens into a good forest drive and the GR comes out level with a huge quarry on the right (some 1,500 metres from the fork). The track then crosses a small valley and emerges on to a narrow road. Follow this to the left for about 800 metres as far as a pronounced bend to the left.

Detour *20 mins*
Limejouls
Keep along the road and cross the stream. As you go round the bend climb up to the left to the hamlet and chapel of Limejouls.

The GR6 leaves the road for a paved track opposite, which takes you into Roucal.

Detour *45 mins*
Viviers
About 600 metres to the south at the village of Viviers, you can get coaches on the Souillac-Sarlat route.

CARLUX
🏠 ✗ 🍷 ⚓
Château dating from the 13th and 14th centuries.

Detour *40 mins*
ROUFILLAC
🏠 ✗ ⚓ 🚌
Turn south onto the D61, for the small village about 2.5 kilometres from Carlux.

8Km
2

Cross the D61 road and continue on a paved track going down to a little valley which you cross. At the foot of the hill the track goes back up to the right towards a minor road. Cross it and go up a cart track which gives some lovely views over the Dordogne valley and surrounding hills as it climbs. The footpath brings you to the tarmac track for Leuil-de-Lacoste, turn on to it heading right for about 400 metres as far as an intersection. Keep straight ahead on a narrow road past the farms at La Chapelle. In another 400 metres take a track on the left and head south-west until you come to the D61 road, turn left and continue into Carlux.

Leave heading south along the D61 road. Leave it 200 metres beyond the post office and go on to a cart track which goes down to the right. The pathway crosses the little valley and goes up to the La Garénie farms where it meets a tarmac track. A short way beyond this, you will come to a fork where there is a wayside cross. Ignore the right-hand tarmac track and keep straight on heading west. The track begins as tarmac, becomes paved and is eventually a dirt road. It heads west to Leuil-Lagarde. On a level with the farms the GR goes for a short distance along the tarmac track from Le Vignal to Le Ponteil then continues, still heading west, along another tarmac track. Cross a road and in another 500 metres go to the right along a narrow path in the forest which brings you to the hamlet of Les Veyssières.

The track goes along past a farm and emerges on to a minor road down which you go left to a fork. Take a cart track on the right, down to some fields and the narrow road from Homond to Malevergne, on to which you turn left. On a level with the Château du Paluel, turn right. Cross the Enéa stream and, a little further on, level with the woods, go left to a tumbledown shack. Behind this a poor forest path goes up to the west. At the top of the hill, turn left on to a forest path and down into the little valley of Le Communal.

LE COMMUNAL
Ä

Detour 15 mins
MALEVERGNE
Ä Ÿ ♨
About 1 kilometre to the southeast, at the hamlet of Malevergne is the junction with footpath GR64b.

7Km
1:45

SARLAT-LA-CANÉDA
Ⓗ △ Ä ✖ ♨ 🚌 🚆
ℹ

Town centre has perhaps the best preserved and widest range of medieval and Renaissance architecture in all France. Drama festival is held in summer and guided tours take place every evening throughout high season. Very busy in July and August; the spring and, in particular, the autumn are the best times to explore the Sarlat region.

At this group of farms, go to the left for 150 metres. This brings you to the new intersection with the GR64a. The latter continues into the valley and is waymarked. For the footpath GR6 to Sarlat, take a forest drive on the right which is mainly out in the open. Gradually the path goes into the trees and overlooks a little valley, then goes along to the left of some meadows.

When the footpath reaches Villarzac hamlet on your left, take the track on the right. At the next intersection in 200 metres, take the left fork. The GR comes to the restored hamlet of Le Maine and keeps going down for 250 metres to a grass path on the right. Follow this up to a tarmac road and turn left. By this winding and attractive route the GR goes up in the direction of La Plane and emerges on to a small road which you follow to the left, and then immediately right, for 500 metres. At the beginning of a wide sweep to the left, go straight ahead down a track between walls to Sarlat-la-Canéda.

The GR6 leaves the town by the Rue de la Calprenède (on the left of the Hotel de la Madeleine). A little further on it crosses the ring road and goes up straight ahead, along by the wall of the College of Saint-Joseph. It comes out onto a small road. The path climbs upwards and at the first fork, turn right and take the road for Argentouleau. This hilltop route gives some lovely views over the valley.

When the path comes out on to the D6 road, go left for 20 metres and go left again up a dirt path through the woods. Not far from spot height 295, the path emerges on to a little road down which you go towards the D6 and cross it. A little over to the left the path takes a short cut through the forest and brings you out to the road again a bit further on. Turn left and when you get to the bend leave the D6 road, heading straight on in the direction of Rivaux farms. In 100 metres turn right on to a paved track which goes towards the woods in a north-westerly direction. The GR then meets up with the D6 again. Turn right, for 20 metres and then go left along a cart track to the edge of the forest. Follow the edge of the forest

10Km
2:50

LA BOUYERIE
⌂ ⋏

This section of the GR6
passes the Cabanes
gauloises de Breuil (Le
Breuil Gaul Huts). These are
dry-stone huts (known
locally as bories) which are
often found throughout the

heading east (right). Level with a little farm (on the right) you come into a clearing. Go along it for 200 metres and at the edge of the forest go left for 30 metres. Look out for the waymarkings on some pylons. The path then enters a wood, coming out at the foot of a huge meadow, below the Château de Campagnac. (In the weeks preceding haymaking it is advisable to use the access road to the château by going round the right-hand side of this meadow.)

A track which is rather patchily waymarked goes up through the meadow and comes out on to a road, on the right of the château. Go round behind the château. Leave the road when you reach the last of the buildings and turn to the left up a forest drive heading west, bringing you to the top of the hill where there is a barn. There is a very open view to the south from this point, which at 302 metres is one of the highest points on the walk. Carrying on in the same direction, the path goes down into the woods to a roundabout where a tall oak tree stands. Turn right. The pathway first heads towards the north, and then gradually bears north-west. As it drops down the trail becomes less obvious, and a compass would be useful. Keep heading north-west and in another 200 metres you will come to an old track which you follow down to the left as far as a stream which is sometimes dry. The path goes through the underbrush and emerges on to a track, heading left (south-west). After about another 20 minutes, leave the track and go to the left across the hollow, then up through a thicket on to the D6 road nearby. Turn right for a short distance along the road and take the tarmac track on the left to the hamlet of La Bouyerie.

The GR crosses the hamlet and comes to a fork. Turn sharp right up an old track through the woods, coming out soon after on to a forest drive which you follow to the right for 2 kilometres as far as the deserted farm of Lafaurie. The pathway then goes down towards the south (left), makes a wide sweep and then goes up into the woods. Just before a stone hut, ignore the track leading off to the region. Here they form a little village and were restored as a film set for the film *Jacquou le Croquant*. They make an intriguing little group in an interesting location.

7Km
2

Château de Commarque

Privately-owned property with keep dating from 12th and 14th centuries; military headquarters and buildings dating from 14th and 15th centuries. The vast defensive enclosure, which once contained a village, is now overgrown with forest. 12th-century chapel. Spiral staircase from first floor to terrace from which there is a splendid view. The keep is built on a rock containing caverns which have been converted into stables (facilities for overnight shelter). At the very foot of the rock is a site of prehistoric finds. **Caution:** *there is a risk of stones falling down into the courtyard.*

Detour *1 hr 15 mins*
Cap-Blanc
This is a circular tour from Commarque; to walk to Cap-Blanc and back only takes about 40 mins.

3Km
0:40

right towards the hamlet of Le Breuil (about 50 metres away), and then just beyond it go up to the left on to a tarmac track. Turn right on to this and go past the 'Cabanes gauloises du Breuil' not far from the spot shown on the IGN map as 'Le Bois Gris'.

Continue down this tarmac track to the hamlet of Le Paradoux. Stay on the road heading west, ignore a road on the right, and at the next fork turn to the right (north) up a tarmac track on to the plateau. Here you meet the Marquay road and head left along it (west). In another 250 metres turn right (north) down the track to the Château de Commarque.

Leave the fortified enclosure, turn right and climb the embankment above the ditch to the west of the château. With the ditch behind you, go through the wood and take a path running parallel to the valley, heading west which takes you past the ruins of Petite Borie. Continue in the same direction and, beyond the farm and over to the right, come to a forest path which you follow through the woods heading south-west. It comes out on the edge of some fields. Skirt round them to the right. Head due west along an overgrown path and in another 100 metres join the access path to La Valade. Turn left and up the road to Sireuil.

Detour see left. Make your way to the track which passes below the chapel and down to the Beune where footbridges cross to the other bank. Turn right. Go along the foot of the hill and come to Laussel cavern where a Venus (carved prehistoric statuette of a female figure) was discovered. Keep on up this track to the D48 road and turn left along it. Go past the château (15th and 16th centuries) to the start

of the Chemin du Cap-Blanc, which leads to the left away from the road. From the Cap-Blanc shelter with its fine frieze of carved horses, go down to the Beune and return to the footbridges from downstream.

SIREUIL

Domed 12th-century church.

Go to the open space behind the church and at the far end on the right, facing away from the church, take an old track down towards the valley. You will have fine views over the Beune from this path as it winds across the hillside. The path goes to the left of some abandoned quarries. When the path brings you to the Sarlat road, turn right and make for Cazelle mill. Go left and down into the mill yard. A little bridge takes you to a causeway across the Petite Beune valley.

As you leave the marsh, turn right. Then in another 20 metres turn left up a clearly waymarked path heading south. The GR then bears south-west, passes an abandoned quarry and goes up through woods to the hamlet of La Mazetie. Take a tarmac track on the right for a few dozen metres. At the next bend ignore the road going down and carry straight on along a paved track heading west. If you turn round you will have a lovely panoramic view of the Beune valley and Sireuil. The track crosses a wood, comes to the hamlet of Le Repaire and keeps going in the same direction as far as the start of a left-hand bend. At that point turn right on to a paved track heading west towards some woods. The path heads downwards, bends to the north-west and comes out in the valley on the Sarlat road at the hamlet of Les Girouteaux, which is built into the cliff. Head left along this road and you pass to the right of the Font-de-Gaume cavern.

Cross the Beune and enter the capital of the prehistoric world.

At this point the GR64 meets the GR46 and GR36.

7Km
2

LES EYZIES-DE-TAYAC

🏠 ⌂ ▲ ✕ ⛴ 🚍 🛈

National Museum of Prehistory, closed on Tuesdays; fortified church of Tayac (12th century); Grand Roc cavern with natural crystallizations; museum of speleology.

The National Museum of Prehistory

The Museum stands on a long, rocky terrace above Les Eyzies. It was established here in 1918, among the ruins of the medieval Château de Tayac, on a site first occupied during the Late Magdalenian period. There are six exhibition halls (introduction with documents and charts, regional collections, tombs, artefacts in bone and stone, cave art), various reserve exhibits and a laboratory storeroom, making it one of the most interesting and informative museums in the world for both the layman and the specialist prehistorian. A statue of primitive Man (not, as is often mistakenly said, of Cro-Magnon man) stands on the edge of its terrace, from where there is a breathtaking view over the surrounding valleys, for so long the haunt of different prehistoric races. Into the distance stretches the cliff-face, its caves and rock-shelters now divested of their ancient secrets. It is well worth setting out on the walk signposted from the museum, for further on there is a magnificent view over the Beunes valley, and you can make your humble pilgrimage to the grotto of Les Eyzies. This cave (also called Richard's Grotto — Grotte Richard) was the source of some breccia fragments containing flints and reindeer bones, which were put on display by a mineralogist in Paris. These fragments were acquired by Edouard Lartet, the palaeontologist, and inspired him to go to Les Eyzies in 1862. There he carried out the first archaeological digs of the main deposits in this prehistoric capital. Later in this same cave, Denis Peyrony, an eminent prehistorian, discovered among other things a large accumulation of colouring materials, which suggested that he may have found a workshop used by prehistoric painters.
For information on opening dates and times: Tel. 53 06 97 03.

ACCOMMODATION GUIDE

The many different kinds of accommodation in France are explained in the introduction. Here we include a selection of hotels and other addresses, which is by no means exhaustive — the hotels listed are usually in the one-star or two-star categories. We have given full postal addresses where available so bookings can be made.

There has been an explosive growth in bed and breakfast facilities (chambres d'hôte) in the past few years, and staying in these private homes can be especially interesting and rewarding. Local shops and the town hall (mairie) can usually direct you to one.

Alban
81250 Alban
⌂
☎ 63.55.81.03

Allas les Mines
⌂
☎ 53.29.22.45

Ambialet
⌂
Route de Valence
Mr Delpoux
☎ 63.56.43.53
⌂
☎ 63.55.32.07

Arcambal
46090 Arcambal
⌂ Le Galessie
☎ 65.35.30.27

Les Avalats
81160 Les Avalats
⌂
☎ 63.55.10.07

Beduer
46100 Figeac
⌂ pech Rougié
Mr Henri Pissot
☎ 65.40.03.47
⌂ La Vaysse
Mr Bacalou
☎ 65.40.01.36
or 65.40.03.43

Berganty
46090 Cahors
⌂ Mas de Rouquette
Mr Jean Galtie
☎ 65.31.25.89

Blanat Le Souci
⌂
Mr Marc Estay
☎ 65.33.63.97

Blis et Born

⌂ chez Mr Grellier
☎ 53.05.33.21

La Borderie
⌂
☎ 53.22.32.62

Bouziés
46330 Cabrerets
⌂ des falaises
☎ 65.31.26.83

Brengues
46320 Brengues
⌂ de la Vallée
☎ 65.40.02.50
⌂ La Ferme du Vieux Moulin
☎ 65.40.00.41

Bretenoux
46130 Bretenoux
⌂ de la Cère
☎ 65.39.71.44
⌂ de la source
☎ 65.38.40.02
⌂ La Croix de Piou
☎ 65.38.42.62

Brugnac
81140 Castelnau de Montmiral
⌂
Mme Bourgarel
☎ 63.33.12.65

Bruniquel
82800 Nègrepelisse
⌂
☎ 63.67.24.91
⌂
☎ 63.76.24.76
⌂
☎ 63.67.25.00

Cabrerets
46330 Cabrerets
⌂ La Pescalerie
☎ 65.31.22.55
⌂ de la Sagne
☎ 65.31.26.62

⌂ des Grottes
☎ 65.31.27.02
⌂ Au bon accueil
☎ 65.31.27.11
⌂ La frite dorée
☎ 65.31.27.04

Cahors
46000 Cahors
⌂ L'Aquitaine
☎ 65.21.00.51
⌂ La Chartreuse
☎ 65.35.17.37
⌂ Hôtel de France
☎ 65.35.16.76
⌂ Terminus
☎ 65.35.24.50
⌂ Wilson
☎ 65.35.41.80
⌂ Cottage Hôtel
☎ 65.21.63.04
⌂ Le Melchior
Place de la Gare
☎ 65.35.03.38
⌂ Le Clos Grand
Laberaudie
☎ 65.35.04.39
⌂ de Douelle
76 rue Clémenceau
☎ 65.35.25.93
⌂ de la paix
Place Saint Maurice
☎ 65.35.03.40
⌂ Le vieux porche
☎ 65.22.24.61
⌂ L'Escargot
5 Boulevard Gambetta
☎ 65.35.07.66
⌂ Aux Perdreaux
Place de la Libération
☎ 65.35.03.50
⌂ L'Arapagous
134 rue Saint Urcisse
☎ 65.35.65.69
⌂ Le Balandre
5 avenue Charles de Freycinet
☎ 65.30.01.97
⌂ La Braserade
77 rue Bergougno

☎ 65.35.73.78
🏠 Bistrot Gambetta
19 Allée Fènelon
☎ 65.22.07.03
🏠 Le Bordeaux
15 Boulevard Gambetta
☎ 65.35.20.05
🏠 La Chartreuse
Saint Georges
☎ 65.35.13.45
🏠 Le Fènelon
Place E.Imbert
☎ 65.35.43.48
🏠 La Garenne
Saint Henri
☎ 65.35.40.67
🏠 Le Mondain
216 Avenue Jean Jaurés
☎ 65.22.22.93
🏠 Marie Colline
173 rue Clemenceau
☎ 65.35.59.96
🏠 L'Orangerie
41 rue Saint James
☎ 65.22.59.06
🏠 La Palais
12 Boulevard Gambetta
☎ 65.35.31.23
🏠 Le Phileo
Place des Consuls
☎ 65.22.32.27
🏠 A la tentation
34 place J.J. Chapou
☎ 65.35.31.44
🏠 Tartatou
28 rue Foch
☎ 65.22.15.01

Cahuzac sur Vère
🏠
☎ 63.33.90.17

Calviac
46190 Calviac
🏠 Le Ranfort a Pont de Rhodes
☎ 65.33.01.06

Cardaillac
46100 Cardaillac
🏠 Chez Marcel
☎ 65.40.11.16

Carennac
46110 Carennac
🏠 Auberge du Vieux Quercy
☎ 65.38.69.00
🏠 Fènelon
☎ 65.38.67.67
🏠 des Touristes
☎ 65.38.47.07

Carjac
46160 Carjac

🏠 Les Roses d'Or
☎ 65.40.65.35
🏠 Le Lion d'Or
☎ 65.40.65.47
🏠 Hôtel Moderne
☎ 65.40.60.21
🏠 Hôtel du Pont
☎ 65.40.67.84
⌂
Place du Foirail
Mme Gras
☎ 65.40.60.56

Castel Merle
🏠 de Castel Merle
☎ 53.50.70.08

Castelnau de Montmiral
81140 Castelanu de Montmiral
⌂
☎ 63.33.14.56

Le Change
⌂
☎ 53.06.00.68

Chapelle de Cazes
⌂ Domaine de Cazes
☎ 65.24.62.30

Concots
46260 Limoge
⌂ du Mesnil
Mr Markham
☎ 65.31.51.96

Cordes
81170 Cordes
⌂ Les Cabannes
☎ 63.56.04.17

Creysse
46600 Creysse
⌂ Le Clombier
Mr Mazuel
☎ 65.38.82.63
or 65.32.21.91
🏠 Auberge de l'Ile
☎ 65.32.22.01

Douelle
46140 Luzech
🏠 Auberge du Vieux Douelle
☎ 65.20.02.03
⌂ Le Barry
Mme Odile Clermont
☎ 65.20.04.21
⌂ Le Souleilhou
Mme Raynal Ressegnier Marguerite
☎ 65.30.91.31
or 65.20.01.88

Duravel

46700 Duravel
⌂ Domaine de la Taillade
☎ 65.36.53.53
🏠 Auberge du Baran
Mr Niouloux Jean Francois
☎ 65.24.60.34

Espagnac Sainte Eulalie
⌂
Mr Delfour
☎ 65.40.00.69

Espedaillac
46320 Espedaillac
🏠 Auberge Beauville
☎ 65.40.55.62

Les Eymaries
⌂ Trologyte
Mr Pareja
☎ 53.06.94.73

Les Eyzies de Tayac
⌂ des Eymaries
☎ 53.06.94.73

Faux
⌂ Le Roc
Mr Aguesse
☎ 53.58.31.30

Figeac
🏠
☎ 65.34.06.25
🏠 des Carmes
Enclos des Carmes
☎ 65.34.20.78
🏠 des Bains
1 rue du Griffoul
☎ 65.34.10.89
🏠 Hostellerie Champollion
51 Allée Victor Hugo
☎ 65.34.10.16
🏠 Hôtel au Pont de Pin
☎ 65.34.12.60
🏠 Courte Paille
12 Place Carnot
☎ 65.34.21.83
🏠 Paramelle
59 Avenue du Faubourg du Pin
☎ 65.34.21.82
🏠 du Pont d'Or
2 avenue Bouyssou
☎ 65.34.00.50
🏠 Terminus Saint Jacques
27 Avenue Georges Clémenceau
☎ 65.34.00.43
🏠 Le Pourquoi Pas
2 Avenue J. Loubet
☎ 65.34.03.28
🏠 de la Halle
☎ 65.34.04.28

211

Frayssinet Le Gourdonnais
⌂ Motel l'Escale
☎ 65.31.08.14
⌂ Le Relais à Pont de Rhodes
☎ 65.31.00.16
⌂ La Bonne Auberge
☎ 65.31.00.02

Gignac
46600 Gignac
⌂ la truffière
☎ 65.37.88.95
⌂ de la Poste
☎ 65.37.70.55

Gintrac
46130 Gintrac
⌂ Aux pêcheurs réunis
☎ 65.38.49.41

Gluges
46600 Gluges
⌂ Hôtel des Falaises
☎ 65.37.33.59
⌂ A la bonne friture
☎ 65.37.33.50

Gourdon
46300 Gourdon
⌂ Bissonnier
51 boulevard des Martyrs
☎ 65.41.02.48
⌂ Hostellerie de la Bouriane
Place du foirail
☎ 65.41.16.37
⌂ de la Promenade
Boulevard de genouillac
☎ 65.41.00.23
⌂ Terminus
7 avenue de la gare
☎ 65.41.03.29
⌂ Le Divan
Place de la Libération
☎ 65.41.09.89
⌂ Le Relais de la Madeleine
☎ 65.41.02.63

Gramat
46500 Gramat
⌂ Le Lion d'or
☎ 65.38.73.18
⌂ de Bordeaux
17 Avenue du 11 Novembre
☎ 65.38.70.10
⌂ du Centre
Place de la Republique
☎ 65.38.73.37
⌂ Auberge du Roulage
1 Avenue louis Mazet
☎ 65.38.71.69
⌂ de l'Europe
8 Avenue Louis Mazet
☎ 65.33.15.55

⌂ de la Promenade
Route de Saint Cere
☎ 65.38.71.46
⌂ Relais des Gourmands
2 Avenue de la Gare
☎ 65.38.83.92
⌂ Le Quercy
23 Avenue du 11 Novembre
☎ 65.38.72.88

Gréalou
46160 Gréalou
⌂ Les Quatre Vents
☎ 65.40.68.71

Les Grèzes
81140 Castelnau de Montmiral
⌂ de la Grésigne
☎ 63.33.12.65

L'Hospitalet
46170 L'Hospitalet
⌂ Daudet
☎ 65.21.02.83

Labastide Murat
46240 Labastide Murat
⌂ Climat de France
Place de la Mairie
☎ 65.21.18.80

Laburgade
46230 Laburgade
⌂ Le Pech
Mme Latour
☎ 65.24.72.84

Lacapelle Biron
⌂
☎ 53.71.64.70

Lacapelle Marival
46120 Lacapelle Marival
⌂ Notre Dame
☎ 65.40.82.76
⌂ La Terrasse
☎ 65.40.80.07
⌂ La Glacier
☎ 65.40.82.67
⌂ Le Relais du Ségéla
☎ 65.40.81.91
⌂ Le Galou
Mme Polge
☎ 65.40.85.46

Lacave
46200 Lacave
⌂ Chateau de la Treyne
☎ 65.32.66.66
⌂ Le Pont de l'Ouysse
☎ 65.37.87.04
⌂ des grottes
☎ 65.37.87.06

Laguépie
⌂
☎ 63.30.21.56
⌂
☎ 63.30.27.67

Laramière
46260 Limoge
⌂
Mr Touvet
☎ 65.31.50.46
⌂
Mr Oules
☎ 65.31.54.07

Lauriere
⌂ La Charmille
☎ 53.06.00.45

Laval de Cère
46130 Laval de Cère
⌂
☎ 65.33.87.25

Lebreuil Montcuq
⌂ Borde neuve
Mr Duflos
☎ 65.22.90.49

Lespinasse
⌂, Ferme Bouyssou
☎ 53.06.98.08
⌂ Ferme Fournet
☎ 53.06.98.23

Limoge
46260 Limoge
⌂ Le Bellevue
☎ 65.24.31.49
⌂
Mr Dubrun Roland
Route de Genevieres
☎ 65.31.50.50

Lisle sur Tarn
⌂
☎ 63.33.35.44

Loubressac
46130 Loubressac
⌂
☎ 65.38.18.30

Loze
82160 Caylus
⌂
☎ 63.67.00.49

Luzech
46140 Luzech
⌂ de l'Ile
Rue du Barry
☎ 65.20.10.09

or 65.20.17.27

Marcilhac sur Célé
46160 Marcilhac sur Célé
⌂
☎ 65.40.61.43

Marminiac
⌂ Le Breil Haut
Mr Garrigou
☎ 65.22.80.56

Marsal
⌂
☎ 63.55.15.05

Martel
46600 Martel
⌂ Le Turenne
☎ 65.37.30.30
⌂ Le Lion d'or
☎ 65.37.30.16

La Mas
⌂
☎ 53.29.68.06
⌂ La Genebre
Mr Jean Guy Philip
☎ 53.29.67.63

Milhac d'Auberoche
⌂ La Vieille Forege
☎ 53.07.50.40

Mirandol Bourgnougnac
⌂ des voyageurs
☎ 63.76.90.10

Monflanquin
⌂
☎ 53.36.47.35

Montcabrier
46700 Puy l'Evèque
⌂ Cavant
Mr Lucien Dupont
☎ 65.36.53.16

Montcuq
46800 Montcuq
⌂ du Parc
☎ 65.31.81.82

Monteils
12200 Villefranche
⌂ Café Miquel
☎ 65.29.62.65
⌂ Couvent des Dominicaines
☎ 65.29.62.69

Montfaucon
46240 Montfaucon
⌂ Rouquette

Mr Tétard/ Mme Lemaistre
☎ 65.31.16.64

Montredon Labessonnie
⌂
Mr Granquier
☎ 63.75.13.92

Montvalent
46600 Montvalent
⌂ Veyssou
Mr Ricou
☎ 65.37.31.80

Najac
12270 Najac
⌂
☎ 65.29.71.34
or 65.29.73.95

Orniac
46330 Orniac
⌂ Espinières
Mr Serge Rasseneur
☎ 65.31.32.17

Pampelonne
⌂
☎ 63.76.32.30

Pasturat
46090 Cahors
⌂
Mme Charazac
☎ 65.31.44.94
or 65.31.40.57

Paulhiac
⌂
☎ 53.36.45.90

La Pénétie
⌂ Montheuil
☎ 53.22.80.53

Penne
81140 Castelnau de Montmiral
⌂
☎ 63.56.31.11

Périgueux
⌂
Boulevard Lakanal
☎ 53.53.52.05
⌂ Institut Rural
7 rue Beaulieu
☎ 53.08.57.16

Pinsac
46200 Souillac
⌂ Le Port de Pinsac
Mr Du Peloux de Saint Romain
☎ 65.37.02.40

⌂ Le Bournet
Mr Jauberthie
☎ 65.32.23.94

La Placelle
⌂
☎ 53.22.80.32
or 53.22.81.28

Pont de l'Arn
81660 Pont de l'Arn
⌂
☎ 63.61.23.31

Pont de Cirou
81190 Pont de Cirou
⌂ Pont de Cirou
☎ 63.76.90.53

Port de la Besse
⌂
☎ 65.45.80.49

Prayssac
46200 Prayssac
⌂ Le Vidal
☎ 65.22.41.78
⌂ Le Corral
☎ 65.22.47.12

Puycelci
81140 Castelnau de Montmiral
⌂
☎ 63.33.13.65

Puy l'Evèque
46700 Puy l'Evèque
⌂ Le Bellevue
☎ 65.21.30.70
⌂ Henry
☎ 65.21.32.24
⌂ Domaine des Cazes
Mme Letarte
☎ 65.24.62.30

Reilhaguet
46350 Reilhaguet
⌂ Le relais Saint Amadour
☎ 65.37.96.00

Rocamadour
46500 Rocamadour
⌂ Beau Site
☎ 65.33.63.08
⌂ du Château
☎ 65.33.62.22
⌂ de la Garenne
☎ 65.33.6588
⌂ Bellevue
☎ 65.33.62.10
⌂ du Belvédère
☎ 65.33.63.25
⌂ Le Lion d'or

☎ 65.33.63.04
(H) Le Relais Amadourien
☎ 65.33.62.22
(H) Le Panoramique
☎ 65.33.63.06
(H) du Roc
☎ 65.33.62.43
(H) Sainte Marie
☎ 65.33.63.07
(H) Terminus
☎ 65.33.62.14
(H) Les Vieilles Tours
☎ 65.33.68.01
(H) Le Globe
☎ 65.33.67.73
(H) des voyageurs
☎ 65.33.63.19
(H) Panoramique
☎ 65.33.62.19
⌂ Mayrinhac le Francal
Mme Odette Delnaud
☎ 65.33.64.85
⌂ Blanat
Mme Estay Philippoteau
☎ 65.33.68.27
⌂ Moulin de Caoulet
Mr Murat
☎ 65.37.97.75

Roussayrolles
81140 Roussayrolles
⌂
☎ 63.56.30.98

Rueyres
46120 Rueyres
⌂ Lavinal
☎ 65.40.85.27

Saint Antonin Noble Val
⌂ Moulin de Roumegous
☎ 63.30.64.47

Saint Beauzile
81140 saint Beauzile
⌂ les Grezes
☎ 63.33.12.65

Saint Cirq Lapodie
46330 Saint Cirq Lapodie
(H) du Sombral
☎ 65.31.26.08
(H) du Causse
☎ 65.31.24.16
(H) La Pélissaria
☎ 65.31.25.14

Saint Etienne de Vionan
⌂ Commune de l'Isle
☎ 63.40.44.55

Saint Geniés
⌂

Mr Delmares
☎ 53.22.84.93

Saint Léon sur Vézère
(H) de la Poste
☎ 53.50.73.08
(H) du Pont
☎ 53.50.73.07

Salviac
46340 Salviac
(H) de la Poste
☎ 65.41.50.30

Sarrazac
46600 Sarrazac
(H) de cartassac
☎ 65.32.13.80
(H) Aussel
☎ 65.37.70.38

Sauliac sur Célé
46330 Sauliac sur Célé
(H) Les Grillons

Souillac
46200 Souillac
(H) les Granges vieilles
Route de Sailat
☎ 65.37.80.92
(H) du Puy d'Alon
Avenue Jean Jaurès
☎ 65.37.89.79
(H) La Renaissance
2 Avenue Jean Jaurès
☎ 65.32.78.04
(H) Les ambassadeurs
7-12 Avenue du Général de
Gaulle
☎ 65.32.78.36
(H) Bellevue
68 Avenue Jean Jaures
☎ 65.32.78.23
(H) de France
62 Boulevard L.J. Malvy
☎ 65.37.81.06
(H) Le Grand Hôtel
1 Allée de Verninac
☎ 65.32.78.30
(H) Le Nouvel Hôtel
21 Avenue du Général de Gaulle
☎ 65.32.79.58
(H) de la Promenade et des
Accacias
12 Boulevard L.J. Malvy
☎ 65.37.82.86
(H) Le Quercy
1 rue de la Récège
☎ 65.37.83.56
(H) Roseraie
42 Avenue de toulouse
☎ 65.37.82.69
(H) La Vieille Auberge

☎ 65.32.79.43
(H) La Cascade
rue de Timbergues
☎ 65.37.84.49
(H) Auberge du puits
5 place du puits
☎ 65.37.80.32
(H) Le Périgord
31 Avenue Général de Gaulle
(H) Le Redouille
28 Avenue de Toulouse
☎ 65.37.87.25
(H) Auberge des Tilleuls
Pas de Raysse
☎ 65.32.72.59

Tanus
81190 Tanus
(H) des voyageurs
☎ 63.76.30.06
(H) du Nord
☎ 63.76.37.38

Thémines
46120 Thémines
⌂
Mr Michel Lacarrière
☎ 65.40.85.03

Touzac
46700 Touzac
(H) La Source bleue
☎ 65.36.52.01

Trébas
⌂
Mr Caza
☎ 63.55.93.92

Varaire
46260 Limoge
⌂ Fontvieille
Mr Lamouroux
☎ 65.31.52.34
⌂ Pech Olié
Mr Bernard Serre
☎ 65.31.59.57

La Védillerie
81170 Cordes
⌂
Mr Kerjean
☎ 63.56.04.17

Vezac
⌂
⌂ Les Cabannes
Mr Galon
☎ 53.29.52.28

Villefranche de Rouergue
12200 Villefranche
⌂ Promenade de Giraudet
☎ 65.45.13.18

INDEX

Details of bus/train connections have been provided wherever it was possible. We suggest you refer also to the map inside the front cover.

Aiguille du Cingle 183
Allas-les-Mines 78
Andole 27
Angoulême 25
  Puymoyen, No. 8 departs from Place du Champs de Mars hourly except Sundays)
Arcambal 108
  Cahors to Villefranche-de-Rouergue
Auberoche 56
Aujols 108

Bach 117, 173
  Cahors (infrequent)
Beauregard 119
  Cahors
Bédeur 181
Bégoutte 135
Belvès 79
  Office de Tourisme, Place d'Armes
Bertoux (Les) 195
Beynac 39
Biron 87
Blanat-le-Souici 193
Blis-et-Born 56
Bonaguil 90
Bouillac 83
Boulouneix 37
Bourdeilles 45

Bouyerie (La) 204
Bouziès 112
  Cahors to Capdenac
Brantôme 39, 45
  Périgueux to Angoulême
  Office de Tourisme, Pavillon Renaissance
  53.05.80.52.
Brugnac 141, 144
Bruniquel 149

Brussac 47

Cabannes (Les) 135
Cahors 105, 107, 169
  Paris to Spain, Bordeaux to Rodez
  Fumel to Libos,

Capdenac
  Office de Tourisme, Place Aristide-Briand
  65.35.09.56.
Cahuzac-sur-Vère 137

Cajarc 178
  Cahors to Capdenac
  Office de Tourisme, Place Foirail
  65.40.72.89.
Cap-Blanc 205
Cardaillac 189
  Figeac
Carlux 201
Castel Merle 69
Castelfranc 99
  Cahors – Monsempron – Libos
Castelnau-de-Montmiral 139
  Office de Tourisme, 81140 Castelnau-de-Montmiral
  63.33.13.65.
Caussade 52
Cayla (Le) 137
Caylus 163

Cazals 160
Champagnac-de-Belair 39
Champcevinel 51
Chancelade 48
  Périgueux
Change (La) 56
  Laribière
Château de Beauregard 33
Château de Commarque 205
Château de l'Herm 61
Château de la Filolie 65
Château de Puyguilhem 39
Château des Bories 54
Coly 67
Communal (Le) 203
Concots 114
Cordes 135, 157
  Montauban
  Office de Tourisme, Maison de Grand Fauconnier
  63.56.00.52.
Corniche de la Belle 35
Coste (La) 117
Coustous 137, 157

Croix de la Rebière (La) 58
  Périgueux-Brive, Périgueux-Thenon-Montignac -Sarlat line
  53.08.69.55.
  Laribière, Périgueux
  53.08.05.75.
Crozes (Les) 157

Douelle 103
  Cahors to Libos
Duravel 93
  Cahors to Libos
  65.36.50.01.

Edon 31
Eyzies-de-Tayac (Les) 73, 75, 208
  Office de Tourisme, Place Mairie
  53.06.97.05.

Fanlac 63
Faycelles 183
  Figeac to Cahors
Figeac 183
  Paris, Toulouse, Aurillac
  Cahors, Decazeville, Toulouse
  Office de Tourisme, Place Vival
  65.34.06.25.
Fongauffier 79
Fouquebrune 27

Gaillac 176
Galessie-Bas 108
Gourdoux 52
Gramat 191
  Office de Tourisme, Place République
  65.38.73.60.
Gréalou 181
  Cajarc to Figeac
Grèzes (Les) 159

Jasse (La) 144
Jean-de-Bannes 83

Lac Nègre 61
Lacapelle-Biron 87

Lacapelle-Marival 189
🚌 Cahors, Saint Céré,
Figeac, Latronquière, Assier
🅱
☎ 65.40.81.11.
Lacave 195
Lafarge 39
Laguépie 131
🚌 Montauban
🅱
Laramière 121
Laurière 54
Laval 141, 144
Leguillac-de-Cercles 35
Lespinasse 70
L'Hopital de Beaulieu 191
Limejouls 199
Limogne-en-Quercy 174
Lisle-sur-Tarn 142, 147
🅱
Loc-Dieu Abbey 121
Loze 167
Luzech 100
🚌 Cahors to Libos
🅱 ☎ 65.30.72.32.

Madeleine (La) 70
Malevergne 203
Mareuil 33
🚌 Angoulême to Périgueux
🅱
Marnaves 155
Mas de Dégot 117, 173
Mas de Vers 173
Mas del Pech 176
Mazaurie (La) 43
Mazuts (Les) 109
Mergieux 131
Merlande Priory 47
Milhac-d'Auberoche 61
Monpazier 85,
🚌 Bergerac, Périgueux
🅱
Montaigut 142
Montarels (Les) 147
Monteils 124, 127
🅱
Montferrand-du-Périgord 83
Montignac 65
🅱 Office de Tourisme,
Place Bertran-de-Born
☎ 53.51.82.60.
Moulin De Caoulet 195
Moustier (Le) 70
Mouthe (La) 75

Najac 131
🚌 Villefranche
🅱 Office de Tourisme,
Place Faubourg
☎ 65.29.72.05.

Parisot 129
🚌 Montauban to Rodez
Pasturat 111
Paussac-Saint-Vivien 37
Pech Grignal 152, 160
Penne 151, 160
🅱
Périgueux 48
🚌 Limoges, (change for
Paris, Lyon, Strasbourg),
Bordeaux, Brive (change for
Toulouse)
🅱 Office de Tourisme,
1 Avenue Aquitaine
☎ 53.53.10.63.
Pinsac 196
Plane (La) 117, 174
Pont de la Peyre 195
Pont du Moulin du Saut 193
Pontaroux (Le) 29
Prayssac 99
🚌 Cahors to Libos,
Cahors to
Villefranche-du-Perigord
🅱 ☎ 65.22.40.57.
Puech (Le) 121
Puy l'Evêque 95
🚌 Cahors to Libos
🅱 ☎ 65.30.81.45.
Puycelci 141
🅱 Office de Tourisme,
81140 Castelnau-de-
Montmiral
☎ 63.33.13.65
Puymoyen 25
🚌 Angoulême

Quina (La) 29

Refuge Eaux Claires 25
Rocamadour 195
🚌 Souillac, Gramat
(during school times)
☎ 65.33.62.12
🅱 ☎ 65.33.62. 59
Rochebeaucourt et Argentine
(La) 31
🚌 Périgueux,
Angoulême, Mussidan
Roufillac 201
Rudelle 189
Rueyres 191

Saint-Amand-de-Coly 67
Saint-Antonin-Noble-Val 163
🚌 Montauban to Albi
🅱
Saint-Bressou 189
Saint-Cirq-Lapopie 112
🚌 Cahors to Capdenac
🅱
Saint-Cyprien 77

Saint-Etienne-de-Vionan 144
Saint-Front-sur-Lémance 89
🚌 Paris to Agen
🅱
Saint-Gringaud 85
Saint-Jean-de-Côle 39
Saint-Jean-de Laur 176
🚌 Cahors to
Villefranche-de-Rouergue
Saint-Léon-sur-Vézère 69
Saint-Martin-le-Redon 91
Saint-Projet 167
Saint-Saud-Lacoussiére 43
Saint-Vincent-Rive-D'Olt 100
Salvagnac 145
🅱
Sarlat-la-Canéda 203
🅱 Office de Tourisme,
Place Liberté
☎ 53.59.27.67
Savignac 121
Sireuil 207
Sivens Stream 141, 144
Souillac 196
🚌 Saint-Denis-Près to
Martel, Gourdon, Brive, Sarlat
🅱 Office de Tourisme,
Boulevard L.-J. Malvy
☎ 65.37.81.56.

Terrasson-la-Villedieu 67
🅱
Themines 191
Thonac 69
Tournesou 29
Tumulus of Saint-Salvy 147
Tursac 71

Valeuil 45
Vallon des Eaux Claires 25
Vaour 152
Varaire 117, 173
🚌 Cahors to Limogne
(certain days)
Védillerie (La) 135, 157
Verdier (Le) 178
Verrerie (La) 35
Vers 111
🚌 Cahors, Figeac,
Saint-Céré
Vieil Four 160
Vieux-Mareuil 35
Vignéras 51
Villebois-Lavalette 29
Villefranche-de-Rouergue 123
🅱 Office de Tourisme,
Promenade de Guiraudet
☎ 65.45.13.18.
Viviers 201
🚌 Souillac to Sarlat